in the Kennedy Kitchen

Henrietta
Enjoy the Book
all the Best
Neil 2007

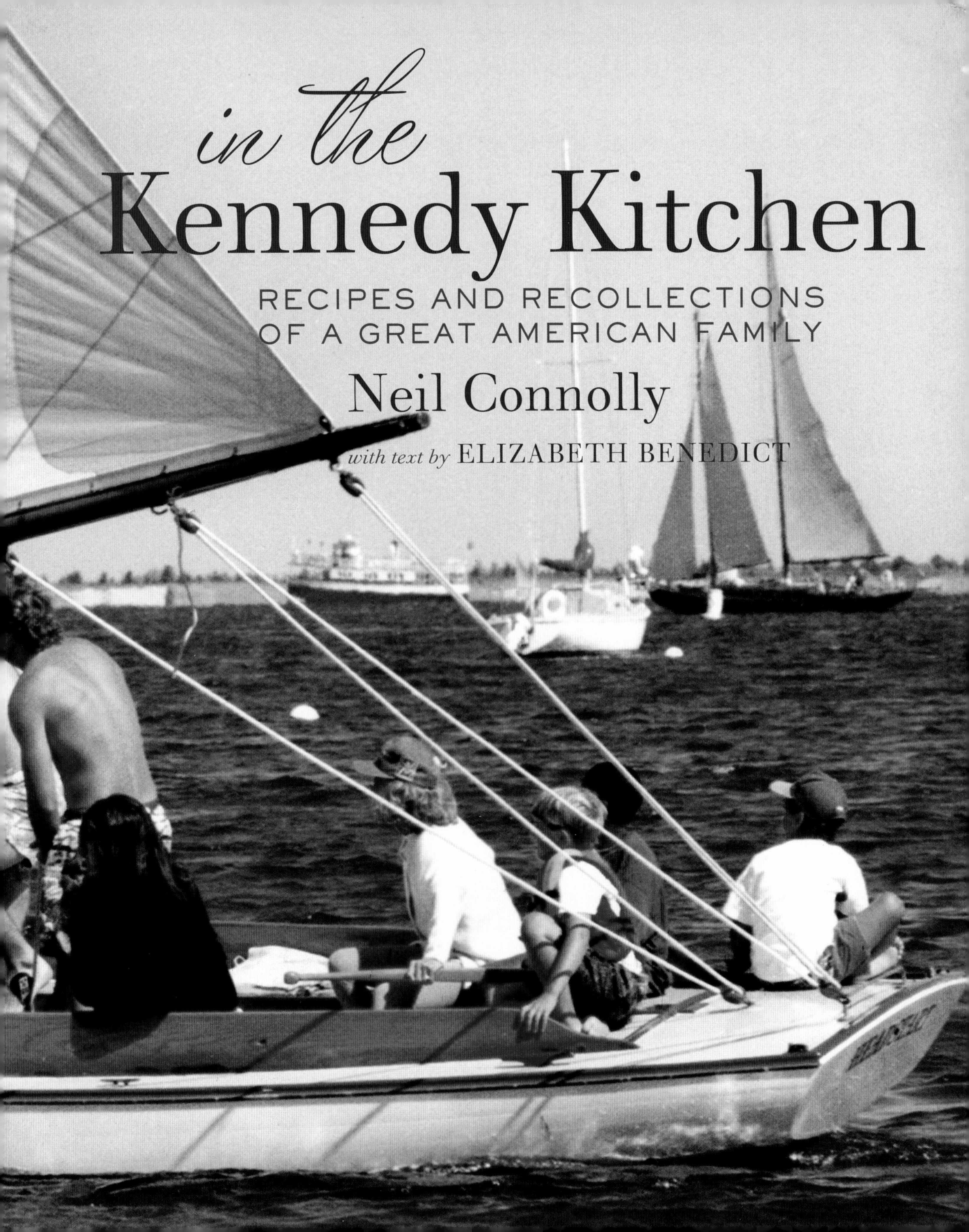

in the Kennedy Kitchen

RECIPES AND RECOLLECTIONS OF A GREAT AMERICAN FAMILY

Neil Connolly

with text by ELIZABETH BENEDICT

London, New York, Munich, Melbourne, and Delhi

SENIOR EDITOR Anja Schmidt
MANAGING ART EDITOR Michelle Baxter
ART DIRECTOR Dirk Kaufman
DTP COORDINATOR Kathy Farias
PRODUCTION MANAGER Ivor Parker
EXECUTIVE MANAGING EDITOR Sharon Lucas
PUBLISHER Carl Raymond

PACKAGED BY King Hill Productions
DESIGN BY Vertigo Design
FOOD STYLIST Alison Attenborough
FOOD ASSISTANT Lillian Kang
PROP STYLIST Barbara Fritz
ALL FULL-PAGE FOOD PHOTOGRAPHY BY Ben Fink

Published by DK Publishing, Inc., 375 Hudson Street, New York, New York 10014

07 08 09 10 10 9 8 7 6 5 4 3 2 1

A catalog record for this book is available from the Library of Congress.

ISBN 978-0-7566-2642-6
Color reproduction by Colourscan, Singapore
Printed and bound in China by Hung Hing

Discover more at www.dk.com

Contents

American Dreams

The family name exists in a realm of legend, history, allure, and deep, abiding affection.

Lucky for us, we now have Neil Connolly's wonderful recipes, photographs, and reminiscences of his many years working on the Kennedy compound in Hyannis Port, Massachusetts, from 1983 to 1995, to remind us anew of what the family has always meant to us.

The Kennedys are our version of royalty, and for a thousand days, what feels like a thousand years ago, four of them made up our most beloved First Family. From out of the stodgy 1950s, Jack and Jacqueline Kennedy burst into the new decade like a meteor shower. They promised new ambitions and dreams for America, and as this new vision took shape and found its trajectory, the glamorous young couple offered us, in the meantime, their radiant good looks, their style and sparkling wit, and two irresistible children romping through the Oval Office—the first youngsters born to a first family since the start of the twentieth century. They were so photogenic and comfortable in front of the cameras, husband and wife, and so generous with themselves, it was as though movie stars had taken up residence at 1600 Pennsylvania Avenue.

The young President—forty-three when he took office—and the even younger First Lady, twelve years his junior, were romantic figures in an innocent age. He had been wounded in battle during World War II, and his older brother had given his life in the war. Their belief in service to the country was as deep as their religious convictions. They were cultured and stylish in a way that made us certain the dreary 1950s were over—and that Jackie Kennedy's sophisticated 1960s were going to be a lot more fun. The President invited Pablo Casals to play the cello at a state dinner. His wife hired a French chef for the White House kitchen and enlisted Oleg Cassini to design her entire

wardrobe—some 300 outfits—with a distinctive look, differing from other First Ladies who used a variety of couturiers.

"We are on the threshold of a new American elegance," Mr. Cassini was quoted as saying at the time, "thanks to Mrs. Kennedy's beauty, naturalness, understatement, exposure and symbolism."

But as privileged as they were, the First Family had a special gift. They always seemed to be inviting ordinary Americans into their extraordinary lives. One day on television, we took a tour with Mrs. Kennedy of the meticulously restored White House. Another day, in *Life* or *Look* magazine, there was a photo album—the loving parents with their children on the floor of the living room in Hyannis Port. The following week on television we caught a glimpse of a dozen hale and hearty Kennedys playing touch football on the famous compound lawn.

We would never own houses in Hyannis Port or become President of the United States, but we nevertheless felt that this First Family belonged to us and we to them. Along with the glamour they projected, they managed to make us feel that they had our best interests at heart. We responded, as people did all over the world, by being utterly smitten with them. We were enchanted and grateful to be observers of their charmed lives, the endless summers on the Cape, the fairytale presidency, the man who would lead us nobly into the New Frontier.

In 1961, the President and French-speaking First Lady traveled to Paris, where she dazzled President de Gaulle and his countrymen—and outshined her escort. The charm of her husband's remark, "I'm the man who accompanied Jacqueline Kennedy

ABOVE LEFT: *John F. Kennedy and his wife, Jacqueline Kennedy, with two-year-old Caroline on the lawn of Rose's house in Hyannis Port, 1961.*
ABOVE RIGHT: *John F. Kennedy and Jackie sailing out of Hyannis Port Harbor on his boat the* Victura, *1961.*

ABOVE LEFT: *John Jr. and wife, the former Carolyn Bessette, on a cold-weather sail with uncle Ted aboard the* Mya.
ABOVE RIGHT: *Pink-and-white striped tents set up along with beach for Rose's 100th birthday celebration, with the Kennedy Compound visible behind.*

to Paris," tipped the popularity scales back slightly in his direction. The night forty-nine Nobel laureates visited the White House, the President won a few more hearts with his wit: "This is the most extraordinary collection of talent, of human knowledge that has ever gathered in the White House," he said, "with the possible exception of when Thomas Jefferson dined alone."

But it was the startling exhortation at the heart of JFK's inaugural address in 1961—"Ask not what your country can do for you, ask what you can do for your country"—that announced the new direction in which he yearned to lead the country. He started the Peace Corps, averted nuclear war with the Soviet Union, challenged racist politicians and policies in the deep South, and set our sights sky high when he vowed we would reach the moon by the end of the decade.

Mrs. Kennedy established a school for the children of White House employees and taught there one day a week; brought writers, modern dancers, and haute cuisine to the White House; and traveled the world as our most prominent good-will ambassador.

While Washington captivated world leaders and policy makers, it was the family's summer residence on Cape Cod, in the exclusive village of Hyannis Port, that became synonymous with the entire Kennedy clan. The secluded six-acre compound, overlooking the jewel-like blue-green waters of Nantucket Sound, came to represent the President's vast extended family in campaign mode and in vacation mode, hard at work and hard at play—sailing, tennis, touch football, the President and his advisors crisscrossing the grounds in their stately suits and ties. These images were soon symbols of what it meant to be a Kennedy. It was on the compound's manicured lawns and in

the grand seaside homes where the family awaited election returns, celebrated political victories, weddings, the births of their children, and where they gathered for comfort during the dark times that are also linked to their name.

During the thousand days the First Family was ours, very few of us got to walk the beach at Hyannis Port or breathe the salty sea air, but our glimpses of family life there made it vibrant and real, and reminded, always, of the power of blood ties. And of the magic of summer days, of our own times at the beach, our cookouts, picnics, and cherished family gatherings.

The Kennedys were very different from us, but they were also the embodiment of what it meant to be American. They were the descendants of impoverished immigrants, people who had fled Ireland in the 1860s, escaping poverty and the potato famines, only to arrive in the closed, snobbish society of Brahmin Boston, where the Irish were despised. Only in America could people on the margins work their way to the centers of power, to Harvard and the White House, in two or three generations.

So many of us have grown up with the Kennedys, we probably know as much about their family history as we know about our own. We have been rapt witnesses to their children's births, their weddings, their moments of glory, and to too many of their funerals.

Looking back on the half-century of books and the countless photographs and precious video clips that remain of Jack and Jackie and their children, I try to resist feeling sorrowful over all they've lost—and we've lost. I prefer to think of them in the place where they were happiest: at their cherished family retreat in summer.

ABOVE: *Rose Kennedy's House.*

BELOW LEFT: *Jacqueline Kennedy Onassis and her son, John Jr. at Maria Shriver's wedding.*
BELOW RIGHT: *John Jr. and cousins playing touch football in their bare feet in the front lawn of his grandmother's house at the family Compound in Hyannis Port.*

The sparkling water and the deep blue sky stretch out as far as the eye can see. Dozens of moored sailboats bob in the harbor. Others under full sail cut across Nantucket Sound on their way to distant shores. Children are building sandcastles on the beach. A picnic is about to begin. That evening, the grownups will have an elegant dinner and lively conversation. But now, at the edge of the water with their sons and daughters, their siblings, in-laws, nieces, and nephews, life is simple and sweet. The sun is shining, the tide is coming in. I want with all my heart to wish them well.

ELIZABETH BENEDICT
JUNE 2006
BOSTON

FACING PAGE: *Senator Ted Kennedy's schooner, the* Mya, *sailing out to sea.*

An Incredible Journey

Passion, hard work, and a hearty helping of sheer luck—the perfect recipe for landing a chef's job of a lifetime.

For almost 12 years, from 1983 to early 1995, I was the family chef for Rose Kennedy and her son Senator Edward Kennedy, in their legendary summer home on Cape Cod. Located in the village of Hyannis Port, the sprawling beachfront house was the focal point of the family's "Compound," a secluded seaside estate, consisting of several houses, which had gained international fame when it became "the President's summer home," upon John Kennedy's election in 1960. It was the kitchen of the late President's childhood home, the emotional hub of the compound, that was my workplace.

That exclusive destination was never one I sought or even dreamed of. What took me there was my lifelong enchantment with cooking, baking, and feeding people. At the age of fourteen, I had my first kitchen job, working in a Mexican restaurant in San Jose, California. By the age of twenty-seven, I was the executive chef at a Boston-area restaurant. At thirty, I was an accomplished professional chef, trying my hand—and winning—culinary competitions throughout New England. My specialties were pastry, chocolate confections, pulled sugar, and grand buffets. I began to be inducted into prestigious culinary societies throughout the world, from New England to Germany and Austria. Before long, I was cooking and baking in fine restaurants, country clubs, and hotels. My position as executive chef at Dunfey's, a trendy hotel restaurant in Hyannis, not far from the Kennedy Compound, put me in the right place at the right time. I had been hired as executive chef at Dunfey's in 1983 to enhance the restaurant's menus and the hotel's reputation.

One night in early 1983, Senator Kennedy's family chef fell ill. A member of his staff called Dunfey's, and the message came to me. I was asked to fill in and prepare dinner that night—for 60 people. All seemed to go well. The very next day, the Senator's secretary called and invited me to work as the personal chef for the Senator's mother, Rose Kennedy, who by then lived year-round at the Compound in the original family house, and the Senator, who had moved there in the early 1980s.

I'd always been told that when you're offered a job, you should never say "Yes" or "No" right away. But this was no ordinary offer, and my customary reserve fell by the wayside. My name isn't Connolly for nothing! To my Boston Irish family, the late President Kennedy remains to this day on a pedestal with the Pope and Dylan Thomas. I don't know how many seconds it took me to snap out of my mild shock and answer, as steadily as I could, "I'd be very honored."

I soon learned that when you worked at the Compound, you worked for all the Kennedys. My primary responsibility was to Rose Kennedy and Senator Kennedy, who shared the sprawling white clapboard house with the Senator's three children, Patrick, Kara, and Ted, Jr. Each of the other family houses on the compound and nearby had its own cook; but because I was the only professional chef among them, I was frequently asked to pitch in on special occasions—and they were plentiful. I worked closely with Caroline and Mrs. Jacqueline Kennedy Onassis to plan a wedding-week luncheon for Maria Shriver and now-Governor Arnold Schwarzenegger. Two months later, when Caroline got married on the Compound, Mrs. Onassis and I joined forces to see that

ABOVE LEFT: *Neil Connolly completely in command after preparing a memorable 6-course meal at the Beard House, in July, 2006;* ABOVE RIGHT: *Neil with Julia Child, after judging entries at "Let's Eat Cake," a fundraiser for the homeless in Boston in 1989.*

the carefully orchestrated day went off without a hitch. For Rose Kennedy's hundredth birthday party in 1990, I baked the over-sized cake, struggled to light 100 tiny candles, and then watched in delight as grandchildren and great grandchildren helped her blow them out.

In summer, I was in charge of the big Fourth of July clambake for 200 guests—and all the other clambakes, as well as the daily boat lunches served on board the Senator's schooner, the *Mya*, and the menus for his small dinner parties in the dining room overlooking Nantucket Sound, where talk of Washington politics animated the soothing surroundings. I prepared huge meals, feeding hundreds of people for fundraisers, and simple family suppers of poached salmon or broiled scallops for one of the Kennedy sisters and their families: Jean Kennedy Smith or Maria's mother, Eunice Shriver, who founded the Special Olympics, and her husband, Sargent Shriver. In fall and winter, I made elaborate Thanksgiving and Christmas dinners for the family. Thanks to the Kennedys' generosity to their community, I also worked with local chefs providing holiday meals for thousands of school children and seniors.

ABOVE LEFT: *Neil carrying in the whipped cream and berry-filled chocolate cake he baked for Rose's 100th birthday for an intimate family party.* ABOVE RIGHT: *Neil and Kennedy cook Nellie McGrail in Rose's kitchen, getting ready for a big brunch.*

The kitchen where I worked was in the back of the house, so centrally located on the Compound that it was a main thoroughfare for most foot traffic. Family members and visitors usually came and went through the back door of the house, which led directly into my kitchen. Right outside was the spacious Compound parking lot, a view of the swimming pool, and a sliver of Nantucket Sound in the distance. Whether it was Ethel Kennedy or one of her many children, John Kennedy Jr., Jackie Onassis, or

Caroline, they passed through the kitchen on their way to see the beloved lady of the house or their Uncle Ted, or simply to cut through—grabbing a chocolate chip cookie or brownie—on their way to the front door and the porch, which led down a flight of steps to the grand lawn and the beach.

As people do in every family, they often lingered in the kitchen, talking to me and to one another. In their bathing suits, running shorts, and tennis togs, they swapped stories and jokes, showed off new babies, and made plans for sailing, swimming, and tennis. And they did what each of us does in the kitchen where we feel at home: Without an invitation, they would stride across the room to the refrigerator and pull open the heavy door, to see what was in there to eat. I made sure there was always plenty: roast chicken, lobster salad, potato salad, cold cuts for sandwiches, fresh fruits, lemonade, and leftovers. And always a big platter of chocolate chip cookies and brownies.

As I look back on those years, the words "warmth" and "controlled chaos" always come to mind to describe the atmosphere. Closeness and affection emanated from the

BELOW LEFT: *Neil eyeing the set-up for a fundraising dinner in Rose's dining room.*
BELOW RIGHT: *Neil on Rose Kennedy's porch.*

larger-than-life personalities in that larger-than-life clan. The Compound sometimes felt like a country unto itself, alive with an ever-widening assortment of residents and visitors. There was always room for one more—or twenty more—at the table, on the sailboat, or at the clambake. I might come to work in the morning prepared to make a cozy dinner for eight that night. By noon, that had changed to a buffet for forty—while I threw together a half dozen roast chicken sandwiches, three more batches of chocolate chip cookies, and a fresh pot of clam chowder for some hungry kids. A lifetime of working in restaurants and country clubs was excellent preparation for cooking for the crowds at the Compound.

But there was nothing that quite prepared me for the parade of dignitaries, artists, and celebrities who were regular visitors. The revered newsman Walter Cronkite came to see the Senator from his summer home in Martha's Vineyard, and the men always went sailing together (on occasion I was on board, cooking and helping sail.) On other days, I made lunches, dinners, and snacks for senators, statesmen, the Prime Minister of Ireland, Carly Simon and James Taylor, Jane Fonda, and Peter, Paul, and Mary. I cooked for a high-profile event at the Kennedy Library in Boston, for lunches during the Democratic Convention in New York City in 1992, and I accompanied the family on several trips to St. Croix. All in a day's work.

The dishes I prepared for the Kennedys and their compatriots—on land and at sea—bring back my most vivid memories of that extraordinary decade. I'm happy to be able to share them with you.

FACING PAGE: *John Jr. throwing a Frisbee on the beach below the Compound.* ABOVE: *The front of the Compound tented for Rose's 100th birthday celebration.*

Appetizers and Hors d'Oeuvres

The President's House, which JFK and his wife, Jackie, bought in 1956

"In every season, every day of the week, there was always room for one more, or twenty more, at the table. *It was always my pleasure to feed them.*"

Baked Brie Wrapped in Filo with Walnut Glaze

SERVES 12 TO 16 WITH OTHER APPETIZERS

BAKED BRIE, ESPECIALLY ONE THIS SIZE, is a dramatic appetizer to dress up a buffet table and always very popular. I often serve this simply with rounds of sliced baguette, but apple or pear wedges and dates can be arranged around the baked cheese for a really smart-looking presentation.

4 tablespoons butter, melted
4 sheets of filo dough (follow package directions for thawing)
1 (16-ounce) cold wheel of French brie
¾ cup chopped walnuts
2 tablespoons brown sugar

1. PREHEAT THE OVEN TO 375 DEGREES F. Melt the butter in a small saucepan.

2. LAY OUT THE FILO SHEETS on your counter and cover with a moist towel to keep the dough from drying out. Take out one sheet, smooth it flat, and brush evenly with melted butter. Now place a second sheet over the first and brush that with butter. Repeat with the remaining 2 sheets.

3. PLACE THE WHOLE WHEEL of brie in the center of the filo. Starting at one corner, fold the filo up over the cheese, pleating as necessary and folding the pastry all around until the cheese is completely covered. Work quickly so the filo doesn't dry out and crack. Invert the cheese onto a baking sheet so the folded edges are underneath.

4. BAKE FOR 15 MINUTES, or until the pastry is golden brown.

5. WHILE THE CHEESE IS BAKING, return the remaining butter (about 2 tablespoons) in the saucepan to medium heat. Add the chopped walnuts and the brown sugar. Cook, stirring, until the brown sugar caramelizes to a syrup and glazes the nuts, 6 to 8 minutes. Watch carefully and stir often to prevent scorching.

6. REMOVE THE BRIE FROM THE OVEN and carefully transfer to a serving platter. Pour the warm walnut glaze over the top and serve at once.

Cheese Dip with Olives and Roasted Red Pepper

MAKES ABOUT 1¾ CUPS

EVEN IN A RATHER GRAND HOME like the Kennedys', everyone needs a nibble. This easy dip is good with raw vegetables, flat bread, or crackers.

1 package (8 ounces) cream cheese, at room temperature
½ cup crumbled feta cheese
¼ cup grated Parmesan cheese
2 tablespoons mayonnaise
1 teaspoon Worcestershire sauce
1 teaspoon fresh lemon juice
1 garlic clove, crushed
2 tablespoons coarsely chopped roasted red pepper
2 tablespoons coarsely chopped pitted Kalamata olives

1. PUT THE CREAM CHEESE, feta, Parmesan, mayonnaise, Worcestershire, lemon juice, and garlic in a food processor. Blend well.

2. ADD THE ROASTED RED PEPPER AND OLIVES. Pulse until finely chopped and thoroughly mixed.

Garlic-Cheese Crostini

SERVES 8 TO 12

FORGET ABOUT ORDINARY GARLIC BREAD—and forget about calories—this rich appetizer runs away with the show every time I serve it. For a party, I suggest you make a double batch. Cut crosswise into 1-inch strips, the crostini makes a great hot hors d'oeuvre. Cut into larger slices, it's an excellent accompaniment to almost any pasta dish.

1 French baguette
2 to 3 tablespoons olive oil
2 cups mayonnaise
2 cups shredded Swiss cheese (about 7 ounces)
2 cups grated Parmesan cheese (about 7 ounces)
2 tablespoons chopped fresh basil
1 tablespoon minced garlic

1. SPLIT THE BAGUETTE in half horizontally so you have 2 long pieces of bread. Brush the olive oil over the cut surfaces of the bread. Either grill on a barbecue or under a hot broiler to toast lightly.

2. PREHEAT THE OVEN TO 375 DEGREES F. Using an electric mixer or a food processor, blend together the mayonnaise, Swiss cheese, Parmesan cheese, basil, and garlic. Spread the cheese mixture evenly over both halves of the baguette. It will cover in a thick layer (about ¼ inch).

3. PLACE THE BAGUETTE HALVES on a baking sheet and bake for 7 to 9 minutes, until golden brown and bubbling. Transfer to a cutting board and slice crosswise into 1-inch pieces to pass as a hot hors d'oeuvre, or larger if using as a substitute for garlic bread. Arrange on a platter and pass while hot.

Variations

Tomato Crostini: Prepare the Garlic-Cheese Crostini as described above, but after toasting the baguettes, cover the bread with thinly sliced plum tomatoes (about 6) in a single layer before adding the cheese mixture.

Prosciutto Crostini: Prepare the Garlic-Cheese Crostini as described above, but after toasting the baguettes, cover the bread with about 2 ounces of paper-thin slices of prosciutto, trimming and folding the slices as necessary to fit, before adding the cheese mixture.

Artichoke Crostini: Drain a 12-ounce jar of marinated artichoke hearts. Thickly slice the hearts. Prepare the Garlic-Cheese Crostini as described above, but after toasting the baguettes, cover the bread with the artichoke slices before adding the cheese mixture.

WELCOME TO THE COMPOUND

There was nothing complicated about what happened in the spring of 1926, in the midst of the roaring '20s, when Joseph and Rose Kennedy rented a grand beachfront summer cottage on Cape Cod. In the years before, they had rented houses in Maine and later in the South Boston resort of Cohasset, home to many of Boston's wealthy Brahmin families. But even though Rose was the daughter of Boston's former mayor, and therefore "high Irish," prejudice against the Irish was virulent, and the family was not at all welcomed there. They continued southward and east, onto Cape Cod, choosing to rent in the secluded village of Hyannis Port, down the road from the town of Hyannis. Its other residents were also affluent, but their money was newer, like Joe Kennedy's, and local snobberies were not as deep or consuming.

The stately white clapboard rental was a stone's throw from the sparkling waters of Nantucket Sound, from the beach and sand dunes, and from Hyannis Port Harbor. From the long wooden pier in the harbor, Kennedys of all ages launched the sailboats and motorboats that have always engaged and animated them. Renting this secluded

"The stately white clapboard rental was a stone's throw

from the beach and sand dunes, and from Hyannis Port harbor. "

summer house may have seemed like a simple transaction for the Kennedys, but it was one whose repercussions would ripple throughout the century.

After three summers of renting, Mr. Kennedy bought the place for a price thought to be $25,000—considered a bargain, even then—and promptly hired workers to enlarge and remodel it for his nine children. One addition was a theater in the basement, the first private "talking-picture apparatus" in New England. The cost was about $15,000.

The Kennedys' affinity for sailing and racing sailboats began early in their time on the Cape. The first sailboat appeared in 1927; it was named the *Rose Elizabeth* by the two oldest children, Joe Jr., and John, the boy who would become President. Legends about their sailing skills—and their initiative—began when the two boys, aged twelve and ten, saw from the veranda of the house an overturned boat in the harbor. They promptly set sail on the *Rose Elizabeth* to save the man they found hanging onto his vessel for dear life. The Boston Post called the event a "daring rescue," rather exaggerating the endeavor. The early article presaged a lifetime of public attention and acclaim.

Decades later, once Jack Kennedy became a member of Congress in 1952, and after he married Jacqueline Bouvier in 1953, he was constantly in the public eye. Much in need of time away from the spotlight, when he needed privacy and revival, he retreated to his parents' house in Hyannis Port. In 1956, he and his wife purchased a shingled summer house on Irving Avenue, 300 feet from the original

FACING PAGE: *Rose and Joseph Kennedy Sr.'s great white house overlooking the beach, the main building at the Compound, referred to as the "Big House."*
ABOVE: *Ethel Kennedy's summer house in Hyannis Port.*

family dwelling. So began the acquisition of six exclusive acres now known as "The Compound." Today it consists of three houses: the grand original house, known when Rose and Joe Kennedy were alive, as "The Big House," now home to Senator and Mrs. Victoria Kennedy and their many children; the summer home of Ethel Kennedy, where family and staff congregated the night Jack Kennedy won the presidency; and the Irving Avenue property, always known as "The President's House," which was recently sold by Caroline Kennedy Schlossberg to her Uncle Ted.

There are several other homes within walking distance that are owned by other siblings and family members. They belong to Eunice Kennedy Shriver and her husband Sargent; Jean Kennedy Smith; Pat Kennedy Lawford; and Joan Bennett Kennedy, former wife of the Senator.

Connecting the houses and the many members of the family are the spacious emerald green lawns where generations of Kennedys have played touch football, soccer, and Frisbee; the wide sandy beach, and the nearby harbor, where the *Rose Elizabeth* was once docked. Today, this is the home port for a number of Kennedy sailboats and speedboats. Senator Kennedy's beloved schooner, the *Mya*, is his home away from home.

It was my great privilege to work on the Compound, in "The Big House," for over twelve years as personal chef to the Senator and his mother, Rose Kennedy, who lived to be 104 years old. In that decade, I came to know the breathtaking landscape, the faces and culinary fancies of this great American family, and the daily delights and challenges of cooking for an ever-expanding crowd. It was a huge, engaged, interconnected web of cousins, in-laws, grandchildren, amazing aunts and uncles, and friends and colleagues from around the globe. In every season, every day of the week, there was always room for one more, or twenty more, at the table. It was always my pleasure to feed them.

"It was my great privilege to work on the Compound, in "The Big House," as personal chef to the Senator and his mother, Rose Kennedy."

Jack and Jackie cutting the cake at their wedding on September 12, 1953.

Stuffed Mushrooms

MAKES 16

BECAUSE OF THE AMOUNT OF ENTERTAINING at the Compound—private and public—with so many visiting celebrities and heads of state, we did many cocktail parties. These stuffed mushrooms were always a hit. Because they are so substantial, you can allow 2 to 3 per person.

16 large white (stuffing) mushrooms

1 package (5.2 ounces) Boursin cheese

⅓ cup finely diced prosciutto or ½ cup crumbled cooked hot Italian sausage

1 package (10 ounces) frozen chopped spinach, thawed

1 small garlic clove, minced

½ cup grated Parmesan cheese

¼ cup fresh bread crumbs

1. PREHEAT THE OVEN TO 375 DEGREES F. Remove the mushroom stems. Wipe the caps clean with a damp paper towel.

2. IN BUNCHES, SQUEEZE THE THAWED SPINACH between your hands tightly to remove as much liquid as possible.

3. WITH AN ELECTRIC HAND MIXER or wooden spoon, blend the Boursin, prosciutto, spinach, garlic, Parmesan cheese and bread crumbs. Divide the mixture into 16 balls and press each ball into a mushroom cap.

4. BAKE FOR 15 TO 20 MINUTES, or until the topping is golden brown. Serve while hot.

Chef's Note: The professional rule of thumb when planning appetizers for a cocktail party is to allow 10 to 12 pieces per person, so how many you need depends upon what else you are serving.

Hyannis Port Crab Cakes

SERVES 4 AS A FIRST COURSE

MOST CRAB CAKES CONTAIN TOO MUCH FILLER. These are just the way the family liked them: pure crab, lightly seasoned. Crab cakes are so popular these days; people eat them as appetizers and main courses. Accompanied by a couple of salads, they make a fine light luncheon dish. The Mango-Pineapple Slaw on page 132 goes particularly well.

Another alternative is to form these into 16 miniature patties and pass them as a hot hors d'oeuvre. Either way, the crab cakes are good plain, with just a squeeze of lemon, though to dress them up, you can top them with a small spoonful of Mustard Mayonnaise or Mango and Papaya Relish (both recipes on page 30).

12 ounces jumbo lump crab meat
2 eggs
2 tablespoons minced shallots
2 tablespoons minced fresh chives
2 tablespoons mayonnaise
1 teaspoon Dijon mustard
1 teaspoon fresh lemon juice
¼ teaspoon salt
⅛ teaspoon freshly ground pepper
1½ cups fresh bread crumbs
Olive oil, for frying

1. PICK OVER THE CRAB, leaving the lumps intact but removing any bits of shell or cartilage.

2. IN A BOWL, beat the eggs lightly. Whisk in the shallots, chives, mayonnaise, mustard, lemon juice, salt, and pepper. Add the bread crumbs and stir to blend well.

3. THEN ADD THE CRAB and fold it in gently, taking care not to break up the chunks of meat. Divide the crab mixture into 8 portions and roll each into a ball. (Flour your hands lightly to prevent sticking, if necessary.)

4. IN A LARGE SKILLET, heat about 2 tablespoons of olive oil over medium-high heat. One at a time, add 4 crab balls and press down gently with a wide spatula to flatten into cakes. Sauté for 3 to 4 minutes per side, until heated through and golden brown. Wipe out the skillet and repeat with more oil and the remaining crab. Serve hot.

Mustard Mayonnaise

MAKES ABOUT ½ CUP

⅓ cup whole-grain mustard
3 tablespoons mayonnaise
1 tablespoon fresh lemon juice
1½ teaspoons Dijon mustard
Splash of Tabasco
Splash of Worcestershire sauce

WHISK TOGETHER all of the ingredients. Cover and refrigerate until serving time.

Mango and Papaya Relish

MAKES ABOUT 2 CUPS

½ cup finely diced red onion
3 tablespoons vegetable oil
1 Granny Smith apple, peeled, cored, and finely diced
1 mango, peeled, pitted, and finely diced
1 cup finely diced ripe papaya
⅓ cup finely diced red bell pepper
⅓ cup finely diced green bell pepper
¼ cup cider vinegar
¼ cup sugar
Salt and freshly ground pepper
3 tablespoons minced fresh chives

1. IN A LARGE NONREACTIVE SAUCEPAN, cook the red onion in the oil over medium heat to soften slightly, 2 to 3 minutes. Add the apple, mango, papaya, and bell peppers. Continue to cook, stirring occasionally, for 2 minutes. Add the vinegar and cook for 2 minutes longer.

2. STRAIN THE MIXTURE over a bowl to catch the vinegary juices. Set the fruits and vegetables aside. Return the juices to the saucepan. Add the sugar to the juices and bring to a boil, stirring to dissolve the sugar. Continue to boil until a slightly thickened syrup forms, 2 to 3 minutes.

3. RETURN THE RESERVED FRUITS and vegetables to the pan, along with any juices that have collected in the bowl. Stir gently to mix with the syrup. Season with salt and pepper to taste. Transfer to a container and let cool, then cover and refrigerate until chilled. Stir in the chives shortly before using.

Steamers

SERVES 4

FOR THOSE WHO HAVE NOT EATEN STEAMERS before, here's how: Remove the clams from their shells. Peel back the dark skin on the neck of the clam and discard. Dip the clam into the broth first, both to moisten and to rinse off any sand that may have gotten stuck, then dunk them into the butter. It doesn't get any better than this. Be sure to put out a bowl or two for shells and other odd bits. And plenty of napkins!

Because the waters around Hyannis Port were so pristine when I cooked there, I always lined the pot with seaweed and added seawater as well to preserve the "fresh from the sea" taste of the sweet clams.

4 dozen soft-shell clams, or steamers
Cornmeal (optional)
Fresh seaweed (the popper kind or kelp; optional)
1½ sticks (6 ounces) butter, melted

1. AT THE FISH MARKET, especially if you call ahead, you can often get your soft-shelled clams already purged and cleaned of sand. If there's any doubt, as soon as you get them home, soak the clams in a bowl of very cold water along with 3 tablespoons cornmeal for 2 to 4 hours.

2. IF YOU HAVE IT, line the bottom of a medium stockpot or a large flameproof casserole with a few inches of seaweed. Add 1½ quarts of lightly salted water, or enough to barely cover the seaweed. Then cover and bring to a boil. (Note: If you don't have seaweed, bring 2 inches of water to a boil.)

3. ADD THE CLAMS, cover tightly, and steam over high heat for 5 to 6 minutes, until the clam shells open. Transfer the clams to a large serving bowl with a large strainer or slotted spoon. Discard any clams that do not open by the time the others are cooked.

4. STRAIN THE BROTH in the bottom of the pot through a sieve lined with a double thickness of cheesecloth. Serve the clams at once, with small, individual bowls of broth and melted butter alongside for dipping.

Clams Casino

SERVES 4 AS A FIRST COURSE, 8 AS A HOT HORS D'OEUVRE

LIGHT AND HIGHLY SEASONED, these might be served as a first course or passed as a hot hors d'oeuvre. We had many parties that spilled out onto the porches in summer, and these clams were very popular.

2 dozen littleneck clams on the half-shell
2 sticks (8 ounces) butter, slightly softened
1 tablespoon minced garlic
2 teaspoons minced shallot
1½ teaspoons Pernod or anisette
1 tablespoon finely chopped parsley
1 tablespoon finely diced red bell pepper
⅓ cup fresh bread crumbs
2 slices of bacon

1. WITH A SMALL SHARP KNIFE, slip the blade under each clam to release the muscle, leaving the clams nested on the half-shell. Cover with a damp kitchen towel and then plastic wrap and refrigerate until ready to cook so they don't dry out.

2. IN A MIXER with the paddle attachment or by hand with a wooden spoon, combine the butter, garlic, shallot, Pernod, parsley, bell pepper, and bread crumbs. Blend well. Turn out onto a sheet of waxed paper and roll into a log. Wrap well and refrigerate until firm, 30 to 60 minutes.

3. WHEN YOU'RE READY TO SERVE, preheat the oven to 375 degrees F. Cut each strip of bacon into 12 pieces about ½ inch wide. Slice the log of seasoned butter into 24 rounds. Put a pat of butter on each clam. Top with a piece of bacon.

4. BAKE FOR 10 TO 12 MINUTES, until the bacon is lightly browned. Serve hot or warm.

Oysters Kennedy

SERVES 4 AS A FIRST COURSE; 8 AS A HOT HORS D'OEUVRE

PREPARATIONS FOR THESE SAVORY OYSTERS are a little complex, but they are great for entertaining because they can be prepared completely in advance and baked shortly before you're ready to serve. We always used Cotuit or Wellfleets, because they were local to the Cape. Choose the freshest oysters you can find at your market.

24 shucked Cotuit or Wellfleet oysters, on the half-shell
1 package (10 ounces) frozen chopped spinach, thawed
3 tablespoons butter
½ cup finely chopped mushrooms (about 4 ounces)
1 large shallot, finely chopped
1 garlic clove, minced
⅓ cup chopped prosciutto
2 tablespoons Pernod or anisette
Light Cheese Sauce (recipe follows)
Salt and freshly ground pepper
½ cup fresh bread crumbs

1. IF YOUR FISH MARKET hasn't already done it, run a small sharp knife under the oysters to loosen them from their shells. Cover with a clean damp kitchen towel and keep refrigerated until you're ready to prepare them.

2. SQUEEZE THE SPINACH with your hands to remove as much liquid as possible. Give it a few extra chops with a large knife to be sure it's in small pieces.

3. MELT THE BUTTER in a medium skillet over medium-high heat. Add the mushrooms, shallot, and garlic and sauté until the mushrooms are lightly browned, 4 to 5 minutes.

4. ADD THE PROSCIUTTO and spinach and cook, stirring, for 2 to 3 minutes longer. If the spinach gives off liquid, hold a lid over the skillet and pour it off. Stir in the Pernod. Add the cheese sauce and season to with salt and pepper to taste. Remove from the heat and let cool; cover and refrigerate until chilled, about 1 hour. (The spinach filling can be prepared up to a day in advance.)

5. ABOUT HALF AN HOUR before you want to serve the oysters, preheat the oven to 375 degrees F. Top the oysters with about 1 tablepoon of the spinach-mushroom stuffing. Sprinkle 1 teaspoon bread crumbs on top of each. Set them on a half-sheet or large baking pan.

6. BAKE FOR 15 TO 20 MINUTES, until the sauce is bubbling and the crumbs are golden brown.

Light Cheese Sauce

MAKES ABOUT 2 CUPS

2 tablespoons butter
2 tablespoons all-purpose flour
1 ¾ cups milk
½ cup shredded Parmesan cheese
½ cup shredded Vermont sharp Cheddar cheese
⅛ teaspoon freshly grated nutmeg
Salt and freshly ground pepper

1. IN A HEAVY MEDIUM SAUCEPAN, melt the butter over medium heat. Sprinkle on the flour and cook, stirring, for 1 to 2 minutes without allowing the flour to brown. Gradually whisk in the milk and bring to a boil, whisking until smooth. Reduce the heat and simmer, whisking often to prevent scorching, for 3 to 5 minutes.

2. REMOVE FROM THE HEAT. Add the Parmesan and Cheddar cheese and whisk until melted and smooth. Season with the nutmeg and with salt and pepper to taste.

IN THE FAMILY KITCHEN

It was Every Kitchen, and it was like no other kitchen in the world. It was a crossroads and a gathering place for world leaders, busy mothers, sunburned great grandchildren, pumpkin carvers, movie stars, folk singers, and a remarkable woman named Rose. She had made the sprawling white clapboard summer house—known among relatives for many years as "The Big House"—her family's home since 1926. When her youngest son, Senator Edward Kennedy, moved in with her in the 1980s, his graciousness and family feeling made the kitchen an even more popular destination. The back door of the house, with the Compound parking lot right outside and the kitchen right inside, was the main entrance for most visitors, whether they were coming to see their grandmother Rose or cutting through the house on their way out to the lawn or the beach.

With all the visitors and special events of summer—clambakes on the shore, formal dinners for forty, family weddings that brought hundreds to the compound—it sometimes felt like Grand Central Station-by-the-Sea. But Rose's kitchen was essentially a family kitchen, the emotional hub of the Compound, an informal place where

"It was a crossroads and a gathering place for world leaders,

ABOVE: *Rose's house, with wrap-around porch overlooking Hyannis Port Harbor and Nantucket Sound, on which we frequently entertained.*
FACING PAGE, TOP: *Chef Neil's chocolate chip cookies: everyone's favorite.*
FACING PAGE, BOTTOM: *John Jr., sitting on dock at Hyannis Port Yacht Club, holding a cousin's baby.*

cousins connected, siblings shared brownies and milk, and dogs sometimes got lucky when food fell to the floor. Regardless of where they were headed, nearly everyone who came through grabbed a brownie or a chocolate chip cookie or two from the platters I could barely keep stocked. It's hard to say which Kennedy appreciated the chocolate chip cookies most, but John Jr. was a serious contender for first place on his frequent

ledge. During the winter holidays, it was a place to warm up with a cup of spiced mulled cider, which had been steeping on the stove all morning. The irresistible smell of the over-sized turkey roasting in the oven drew everyone, even Rose, to my kitchen.

In every season, it was the room where family members felt at home. As people do in every kitchen where they are comfortable, they'd amble across the room and pull open the refrig-

movie stars, folk singers, and a remarkable woman named Rose."

visits to Grandma or on his way to the beach with girlfriend Daryl Hannah and, later on, with his wife, Carolyn.

In the course of a summer day, I might see Ethel Kennedy, John Kennedy Jr., Mrs. Onassis, Caroline Schlossberg, and more Kennedy cousins than I could count. On a Friday afternoon in July, new arrivals would stop by and ask me who was already there, who was expected for the weekend, and what was for dinner. In their shorts and T-shirts, they showed off new babies, munched on cookies, and traded stories and news. In fall, the room was the setting for the Senator's annual family pumpkin-carving contest, with all of the creations displayed later along the porch

erator door. What would they find there? Big bowls of lobster salad, tuna salad, and potato salad, large platters heaped with roasted chicken, and vast supplies of meats, fish, and vegetables waiting to be prepared. On occasion, someone would pull out a cold roast beef, and as everyone gathered around the old Formica table, I'd whip up sandwiches and side salads, and put out baskets of potato chips, rolls, and bread.

This kitchen, my workplace, was a center of activity, energy, and warm family feeling. Whether I was cooking a formal meal or throwing together a bite for an impromptu lunch or picnic on the boat, it was always a lively and exciting place to be.

Barbecued Cajun Shrimp with Melon and Midori Sauce

4 SERVINGS

HOT SPICY SHRIMP PLAY OFF chunks of cool sweet melon for a perfect pairing none of your guests will forget. When I prepared this dish for the Kennedys, I'd turn the melon into a tempura, dipping the chunks in a light batter and frying them briefly.

To grill the shrimp, you'll need 4 sugarcane skewers, which are available in the produce department of supermarkets in some areas. Otherwise, substitute long bamboo skewers, but be sure to soak those in cold water for at least half an hour first, so they don't catch fire over the coals.

12 jumbo shrimp, shelled and deveined
2 tablespoons Cajun spice
⅔ cup barbecue sauce, No-Cook (page 119) or use your favorite brand
2 cups loosely packed baby field greens
¼ honeydew melon, peeled and sliced
Midori Sauce (recipe follows)

1. LIGHT A HOT FIRE in a charcoal grill or set your gas grill to hot. Alternatively, you could use a stovetop grill pan. At the same time, preheat your oven to 375 degrees F.

2. DREDGE THE SHRIMP in Cajun spice to coat. Skewer 3 shrimp on each of 4 skewers. Grill them, turning, until the outside of the shrimp are marked with nice brown grids, but do not cook through, 1 to 2 minutes per side.

3. TRANSFER THE SHRIMP from the grill to a baking dish. Baste them on both sides with about ¼ cup of the barbecue sauce. Bake for 6 to 8 minutes, until the shrimp are just cooked through.

4. MEANWHILE, PLACE a small mound of baby greens on one side of each of 4 plates. Fan out the melon slices alongside the greens. Lay a skewer of shrimp over each portion. Decorate the plate with a small dollop of both the Midori sauce and the remaining barbecue sauce.

Midori Sauce

MAKES ABOUT 1½ CUPS

1 cup sour cream
2 tablespoons heavy cream
¼ cup honey
2 tablespoons Midori (melon) liqueur

WHISK TOGETHER the sour cream, heavy cream, honey, and Midori. Cover and refrigerate until serving time.

Shrimp Cocktail

SERVES 4 TO 6

NO MATTER HOW FANCY FOOD GETS, old-fashioned shrimp cocktail is perennially popular. At the Compound, this simple starter was sometimes served as a first course. Often for parties, I put out huge platters shrimp with bowls of both the traditional cocktail sauce presented here and the Remoulade Sauce on page 43.

20 to 24 jumbo or extra-large shrimp, peeled and deveined
2 tablespoons pickling spice
1½ lemons
2 cups shredded iceberg lettuce
Seafood Cocktail Sauce (recipe follows)

1. IN A LARGE SAUCEPAN, bring 2 quarts of water to a boil. Add the pickling spice. Squeeze the juice from half a lemon into the pot and toss in the rind. Add the shrimp and cook over high heat just until the water returns to a boil, 4 to 5 minutes, or until the shrimp are pink and loosely curled.

2. IMMEDIATELY DRAIN and rinse the shrimp under cold water to stop the cooking and remove the pickling spice. Drain the shrimp well, put them in a bowl, cover, and refrigerate until well chilled.

3. TO SERVE, MOUND THE LETTUCE in each of 4 or 6 large glass goblets or stemmed dishes set on small plates. Hook the shrimp over the rim of the glass. Cut the remaining lemon into wedges and place one on each plate. Spoon some of the cocktail sauce on top of the lettuce in the center. Pass the remainder on the side.

Cocktail Sauce

MAKES ABOUT 1½ CUPS

1 cup chili sauce
½ cup ketchup
¼ cup prepared white horseradish
¼ cup fresh lemon juice
½ teaspoon sugar
½ teaspoon Tabasco sauce, or more to taste

WHISK TOGETHER all the ingredients. Cover and refrigerate until ready to serve.

Handmade Mayonnaise

MAKES ABOUT 1½ CUPS

I KNOW CONVENIENCE IS ESSENTIAL THESE DAYS, but if you haven't tasted homemade mayonnaise in a long time, you may want to pick a weekend morning and give it a try. Actually, mayonnaise only takes a few minutes to whip up. The only trick is to have your egg yolks at room temperature when you begin—you can cover the whole eggs in their shells with warm water for a few minutes to accomplish this—and to add the oil very, very slowly, in drops at first, then increasing as the mayonnaise comes together and thickens.

2 egg yolks
1½ cups vegetable oil
2 teaspoons cider vinegar
2 teaspoons fresh lemon juice
1 teaspoon Dijon mustard
⅜ teaspoon sugar
Salt and freshly ground white pepper

1. IN A STURDY BOWL, whisk the egg yolks to break them up. Continue to whisk constantly while adding the vegetable oil very slowly, in drops at the beginning. Then, when the emulsion begins to form and the mayonnaise begins to thicken, pour in the oil in a slow, thin stream while continuing to whisk constantly.

2. WHISK IN THE VINEGAR, lemon juice, mustard, and sugar to blend well. Season with salt and white pepper to taste. Transfer to a covered container and refrigerate for up to 5 days; the flavor of the mayonnaise will develop if it's chilled for at least several hours before using.

Shrimp Remoulade

SERVES 10 TO 12 AS AN HORS D'OEUVRE

SHRIMP BREAK THE CATERER'S RULE OF THUMB, because everyone loves them so much. Whatever you put out will disappear before you know it. I always allowed 4 to 5 per person. While you can always pass shrimp with classic seafood cocktail sauce (page 40), this classic *rémoulade*, a complexly flavored mayonnaise, makes a more sophisticated alternative. When you're in a hurry, of course, prepared mayonnaise is fine, but to taste the real thing, try my easy "real" mayonnaise.

2 to 3 pounds shrimp, peeled and deveined
2 cups mayonnaise, preferably homemade (recipe page 41)
1 tablespoon fresh lemon juice
4 French cornichons or gherkin pickles, finely chopped
2 tablespoons tiny nonpareil capers
1 teaspoon finely chopped anchovy or anchovy paste
1 teaspoon finely chopped fresh parsley
1 teaspoon finely chopped fresh chervil
1 teaspoon finely chopped fresh tarragon or ¾ teaspoon dried
1 teaspoon chopped fresh chives

1. BRING A LARGE POT OF WATER TO A BOIL. Dump in all the shrimp and cook over high heat until the water returns to a boil, about 5 minutes. The shrimp should be pink and lightly curled. Drain them into a colander and rinse. Transfer the shrimp to a bowl of ice and water to cool them down quickly. Drain, then refrigerate in a covered container to chill through. (The shrimp can be cooked up to a day in advance.)

2. TO MAKE THE REMOULADE SAUCE, in a medium bowl, combine the mayonnaise, lemon juice, cornichons, capers, anchovy, parsley, chervil, tarragon, and chives. Whisk everything together to blend well. Cover and refrigerate the sauce for up to 6 hours before serving.

Chef's Note: Chervil is a lovely delicate herb with a subtle anise taste. It's easy to grow, but not common in stores. If you cannot find fresh chervil, do not substitute dried, which is tasteless; instead add a bit more tarragon and parsley.

"For anyone not from New England, "chowderhead" is a name for people who love chowder of any kind; but it also means something like *knucklehead*, a teasing term of endearment."

Soups *and* Chowders

The Shriver House

Spring Asparagus Soup with Leeks

SERVES 4 TO 6

ASPARAGUS IS ONE OF THE FIRST SPRING VEGETABLES, and I took advantage of the local crop. Lots of family would descend on the house as soon as the weather turned warm. I always made sure there was plenty of soup on hand. This is one of the more elegant ones.

4 tablespoons butter
1½ pounds asparagus stalks, trimmed and coarsely chopped
2 medium leeks (white and tender green), chopped
3 tablespoons all-purpose flour
1 cup dry white wine
4 cups chicken stock
1 cup half-and-half or light cream
Salt and freshly ground pepper

1. IN A LARGE SAUCEPAN or flameproof casserole, melt the butter over medium heat. Add the asparagus and leeks. Stir to coat with the butter, then reduce the heat to low, cover, and cook for about 3 minutes, until the leek is softened and the asparagus is a darker green.

2. SPRINKLE ON THE FLOUR, raise the heat to medium again, and cook, stirring, 1 to 2 minutes. Pour in the wine and bring to a boil, stirring until the liquid thickens. Add the chicken stock and return to a boil, stirring. Reduce the heat to a simmer and cook until the asparagus is soft, about 10 minutes.

3. REMOVE FROM THE HEAT and add the half-and-half. Puree the soup in the pot with an immersion stick blender or in batches in a blender or food processor. Return to the pot and season with salt and pepper to taste. Reheat before serving.

CHOWDER FOR ARNOLD AND MARIA'S WEDDING WEEK LUNCHEON...

For months during the spring and summer of 1986, the compound was all abuzz with energy, enthusiasm, and a larger number of excited Kennedys and Shrivers than usual. In April, Maria Shriver married Arnold Schwarzenegger, and in July, her cousin Caroline Kennedy wed Edwin Schlossberg. The women were maids of honor at each other's weddings.

On the big day for Maria and Arnold, Oprah Winfrey delighted 500 guests in the church when she read aloud, "How Do I Love Thee," by Elizabeth Barrett Browning. Later that day, under a tent on the Compound, Maria honored her parents when she cut into a towering eight-tier cake that was a replica of their wedding cake. The illustrious guest list spanned the political, entertainment, and media worlds of the bride and groom and included Barbara Walters, Diane Sawyer, Abigail Van Buren, and, of course, the entire Kennedy crowd.

The day before, Caroline and Mrs. Onassis hosted the couple in a more intimate, informal setting, at a buffet lunch for eighty in the President's house on the Compound. The meal was served in the sunlit dining room, surrounded by the antiques and family treasures that meant so much to Mrs. Onassis: Windsor side chairs and drop-leaf tables, an 1830 portrait of a sea captain, an assortment of antique pewter, and a collection of painted wood sailboat models. On their way to the dining room, guests passed by a colorful window display of nineteenth century cobalt blue and amethyst Sandwich glass (from the town of that name on the Cape), which she enjoyed collecting.

Once they filled their plates, they took them to small tables set up in the living room and on the porches. The weather was perfect, and the menu was one I had worked on closely with Caroline and her mother for nearly a month. Especially winning was the theme that Caroline created for the event: corn chowder served in "chowderheads" mugs made just for the occasion. There was clearly no pretentiousness; just self-assured style, good taste, and a mischievous sense of humor that ran in the family.

"The weather was perfect, and the menu was one I had worked

In the weeks leading up to the event, I was frequently on the phone with mother and daughter, going over every detail: the menu, flower arrangements, china, silver, and the overall effect they wanted to create—an informal elegance that defined the house and the setting. These were two women with a distinct aesthetic sense, and it was an immense pleasure working with them at every stage. They were meticulous, unfailingly polite, considerate, and enthusiastic about their tribute to Maria Shriver, as she welcomed a new member into the family.

...AND HOW OPRAH STARTED A CHOCOLATE TREND

The results were magnificent. The dining room was as perfectly put together as a stage set. When the guests arrived, the curtain went up, and the festivities began. The first course, fresh corn chowder, was served in the mugs Caroline had had made. Embossed on each was: “Maria and Arnold—Chowderheads.” For anyone not from New England, a “chowderhead”

on closely with Caroline and her mother for nearly a month.”

is a name for those who love chowder of any kind; but it also means something like “knucklehead,” a teasing term of endearment. In this case, a winning touch of good-hearted, Kennedy humor.

There were several desserts, including the ever-present brownies and chocolate chip cookies, but the knockout was an extravagant certerpiece that took me almost two weeks to make: a dark and white chocolate eagle with an extended wingspan of three feet! The bird's head was made of white chocolate, its beak and talons were white chocolate with golden hues, and everything else was dark chocolate. This was not a sculpture poured into a mold. I carved every inch from couverture chocolate that I bought in ten-pound blocks. The real work was forming and etching 800 chocolate feathers, which I attached individually to the body of the eagle with melted chocolate.

After all that work, it thrilled me to observe the guests as they admired that eagle. They gathered around and marveled at the painstaking technique. I was more than a little proud. But then something happened that I hadn't expected. One by one, they couldn't resist the temptation and reached out and snapped off a feather or two to pop into their mouths. And who was one of the first culprits? Oprah Winfrey, a woman known for her good taste—and for her trendsetting. It was the ultimate compliment.

FACING PAGE: *Maria Shriver arriving at the Compound*
TOP: *Maria Shriver and Arnold Schwarzenegger, just after their wedding ceremony, April 26, 1986.*
ABOVE: *Sweet Corn Chowder, page 53, in the original "Chowderhead" mug.*

Dilled Carrot Soup

SERVES 6

KARA KENNEDY ESPECIALLY LIKED THIS SOUP, which I tended to serve when it was cool outside. We grew dill in our little kitchen garden , so I almost always had fresh available.

3 tablespoons butter
1 medium onion, chopped
2 tablespoons all-purpose flour
½ cup dry white wine
1 pound carrots, peeled and sliced
6 cups chicken stock
3 tablespoons finely chopped fresh dill
¼ cup heavy cream
Salt and freshly ground pepper
Sour cream or plain yogurt

1. IN A LARGE SAUCEPAN, melt the butter over medium heat. Add the onion and cook, stirring occasionally, until it is softened and translucent, 3 to 5 minutes.

2. SPRINKLE ON THE FLOUR AND COOK, stirring, for 1 to 2 minutes. Pour in the wine and 1½ cups of water and bring to a boil, whisking until thickened and smooth. Now add the carrots, stock, and 2 tablespoons of the dill. Bring to a boil, stirring often. Reduce the heat to medium-low, cover, and simmer for 15 to 20 minutes, or until the carrots are soft.

3. REMOVE FROM THE HEAT and puree the soup until it is smooth. If you have an immersion blender, you can do this right in the pot. Otherwise, process in batches in a blender or food processor. (The soup can be made to this point up to 2 days in advance. Refrigerate in a covered container.)

4. WHEN YOU'RE READY TO SERVE reheat the soup until hot. Stir in the heavy cream; season with salt and pepper to taste. If the soup seems too thick, thin with a little more wine or chicken stock. Ladle into soup plates and garnish each serving with a dollop of sour cream and a pinch of the remaining chopped dill.

Cauliflower Soup

SERVES 6

CAULIFLOWER IS A BLAND VEGETABLE that makes an excellent soup. Best of all, it cooks up quickly, allowing you to whip up this homemade dish in 20 minutes or less.

1 medium head of cauliflower
4 cups chicken stock
4 tablespoons butter
1 medium onion, chopped
2 celery ribs, chopped
3 tablespoons all-purpose flour
2 cups half-and-half
Pinch of freshly grated nutmeg
Salt and freshly ground pepper
½ cup shredded Parmesan cheese

1. CUT OFF THE LEAVES and thick stem and separate the cauliflower into florets. Rinse well.

2. BRING THE CHICKEN STOCK TO A BOIL in a large saucepan. Add the cauliflower florets. Cook over medium-high heat for 6 to 8 minutes, or until the cauliflower is tender.

3. MEANWHILE, IN ANOTHER LARGE SAUCEPAN, melt the butter over medium heat. Add the onion and celery and cook, stirring frequently, until softened and translucent, 4 to 5 minutes.

4. SPRINKLE THE FLOUR OVER THE VEGETABLES. Cook, stirring, for 1 to 2 minutes. Add the cauliflower with chicken stock and stir well. Bring to a boil, stirring until slightly thickened. Add the half-and-half and nutmeg. Season with salt and pepper to taste. Reduce the heat slightly and simmer the soup for 5 minutes.

5. REMOVE FROM THE HEAT. Either puree the soup until smooth in the pot with an immersion stick blender or in batches with a food processor. Serve hot. Pass a bowl of shredded Parmesan cheese on the side.

Sweet Corn Chowder

SERVES 8 TO 12

THIS EASY-TO-MAKE SAVORY CHOWDER was served at Maria Shriver and Arnold Schwarzenegger's wedding week luncheon, which was hosted by Mrs. Onassis and Caroline and held at "The President's House."

My trick is to cook not just the corn kernels, but the entire corn on the cob, to impart as much flavor as possible to the stock. Then the kernels are cut off the cob and returned to the chowder.

I used to make a gallon and a half at a time. You probably don't need that much, so I've cut the recipe down. Keep in mind, though, the amounts here can be doubled or halved, depending upon the occasion. For a touch of color, garnish with a sprinkling of chopped fresh parsley or minced chives.

2 cups milk
6 ears of sweet corn, preferably the two-toned butter-sugar variety, shucked
6 tablespoons butter
1 large onion, diced
¼ pound thick-sliced bacon, finely diced
¼ cup all-purpose flour
2 cups chicken stock
1 pound red-skinned potatoes, peeled and finely diced
1 cup light cream or half-and-half
Salt and freshly ground pepper

1. IN A STOCKPOT or other large soup pot, combine the milk with 2 quarts (8 cups) of water. Bring to a boil. Add the corn on the cob and cook it for 5 minutes, or until tender.

2. USING TONGS, transfer the corn to a colander. Measure out and reserve 4 cups of the corn cooking liquid; discard the remainder. When the corn is cool enough to handle, cut the kernels off the cob with a large sharp knife.

3. MELT THE BUTTER in a large soup pot or flameproof casserole over medium heat. Add the onion and bacon and cook, stirring occasionally, until the onion is soft and the bacon has rendered its fat, 5 to 7 minutes.

4. SPRINKLE ON THE FLOUR and cook, stirring, for 1 to 2 minutes. Whisk in the reserved corn broth and the chicken stock. Bring to a boil, stirring until thickened slightly. Add the diced potatoes and cook for 5 to 7 minutes, or until just tender. Then add the corn kernels and cream. Reduce the heat to low and simmer for 5 minutes. Season with salt and pepper to taste.

Cream of Tomato Soup

SERVES 6 TO 8

EVERYONE LOVES THIS ALL-AMERICAN CLASSIC, and you have no idea how good it can be until you make it yourself. My version is loaded with smoky bacon and fresh herbs. It was a recipe I always turned to when there were chilly days at the beach.

2 tablespoons butter or extra virgin olive oil
6 strips of bacon, finely chopped
1 medium onion, chopped
1 medium carrot, peeled and coarsely chopped
1 celery rib, coarsely chopped
2 garlic cloves, chopped
⅓ cup all-purpose flour
2 cups chicken stock
2 cans (28 ounces each) Italian plum tomatoes, juices reserved
¼ cup chopped fresh basil
1 teaspoon dried thyme
1 bay leaf
2 teaspoons sugar
2 cups light cream, half-and-half, or milk
Salt and freshly ground pepper

1. IN A LARGE SOUP POT or flameproof casserole, melt the butter over medium heat. Add the bacon, onion, carrot, and celery. Cook, stirring occasionally, until the bacon renders its fat and the vegetables soften, about 5 minutes.

2. ADD THE GARLIC and sprinkle on the flour. Continue to cook, stirring, for 1 to 2 minutes without allowing the flour to brown.

3. NOW ADD THE CHICKEN STOCK, tomatoes with their juices, 3 tablespoons of the basil, the thyme, bay leaf, and sugar. Mix well. Bring to a boil, stirring until the liquid thickens slightly. Reduce the heat to low, cover, and simmer for about 1½ hours.

4. REMOVE AND DISCARD THE BAY LEAF. Puree the soup in batches, bacon and all. Return to the pot and heat until hot. Whisk in the cream. Season with salt and pepper to taste. Serve garnished with a pinch of the remaining basil.

Late Summer Chicken and Vegetable Soup

SERVES 8

WHEN LOCAL VEGETABLES RIPENED IN LATE AUGUST, I took advantage of the bumper crops of zucchini, green beans, and tomatoes to throw together this fresh-tasting soup. Since there was almost always a roast chicken or two on call in the refrigerator, I'd just pull off the meat I needed and throw it into the soup at the last minute. If you don't have any leftover chicken, you could easily dice a couple of skinless, boneless breasts and add them along with the stock. It will give you even more flavor.

2 tablespoons extra virgin olive oil
1 medium onion, chopped
1 leek (white and tender green), chopped
2 carrots, peeled and diced
2 celery ribs, diced
½ cup sliced mushrooms
4 ounces fresh green beans, trimmed and cut into 1-inch lengths
1 cup diced peeled tomatoes, preferably fresh
¼ cup dry white wine
6 cups chicken stock
2 cups diced cooked chicken
2 cups cooked white beans
1 medium zucchini, diced
2 tablespoons chopped fresh basil
1 tablespoon chopped parsley
1 tablespoon fresh thyme leaves or 1 teaspoon dried
Salt and freshly ground pepper

1. IN A LARGE SOUP POT, heat the olive oil over medium-high heat. Add the onion, leek, carrots, celery, and mushrooms. Sauté for 5 minutes, stirring often.

2. ADD THE GREEN BEANS, tomatoes, and wine. Continue to cook, stirring, for 2 minutes longer. Now pour in the chicken stock. Bring to a boil, reduce the heat, and simmer for 10 minutes.

3. ADD THE CHICKEN, white beans, zucchini, basil, parsley, and thyme. Simmer for 5 to 7 minutes, or until the zucchini is tender. Season the soup with salt and pepper to taste.

Chicken Soup with Ribbons of Egg and Cheese

SERVES 4

UNBELIEVABLY SIMPLE AND COMFORTING, this is one of the quickest soups you can whip up. The Italians call it *stracciatelle*, which means "shreds," or more literally, "little rags," referring to the egg. It's a recipe I'd turn to when I needed soup in a hurry.

6 cups chicken stock, preferably homemade (recipe follows)
Pinch of freshly grated nutmeg
Salt and freshly ground pepper
4 eggs
2 teaspoons minced fresh basil or oregano
½ cup shredded Parmesan cheese

1. IN A MEDIUM SAUCEPAN, bring the chicken stock to a boil. Season with the nutmeg and salt and pepper to taste.

2. MEANWHILE, BEAT THE EGGS until blended. Gradually add the beaten eggs to the boiling stock in a thin stream while stirring the soup constantly with a fork or whisk so the eggs form delicate ribbons. The eggs will cook almost instantly.

3. ADD THE BASIL and immediately ladle into soup plates. Sprinkle 2 tablespoons of the Parmesan cheese over each serving.

All-Purpose Chicken Stock

MAKES 3 TO 4 QUARTS

4 to 5 pounds chicken wings
2 medium onions, quartered
2 large celery ribs, thickly sliced
2 large carrots, peeled and quartered
1 large leek (white and tender green), thickly sliced and well rinsed
5 sprigs of parsley
3 sprigs of fresh thyme or 1 teaspoon dried thyme leaves
2 tablespoons black peppercorns
Sea salt

1. RINSE THE CHICKEN WINGS WELL. Place them in a stockpot. Add 4 quarts of water and slowly bring to a boil. Skim off all the foam and scum that rises to the top.

2. ADD THE ONIONS, celery, carrots, leek, parsley, thyme, and peppercorns. Return to a boil, reduce the heat to low, and simmer, partially covered, for about 3 hours. If the liquid evaporates too quickly, add ½ to 1 cup more water

3. SKIM OFF ALL THE FAT and strain the stock through a sieve lined with a double thickness of cheesecloth into a large bowl. Let cool, then refrigerate for up to 3 days or freeze for up to 3 months until needed.

Cape Cod Clam Chowder

SERVES 6

CHOWDER MADE FROM QUAHOGS, large hard-shelled clams, has long been a tradition on Cape Cod. These beauties are actually the same variety as littlenecks (the smallest) or cherrystones, but because quahogs are allowed to mature fully, they develop an intense flavor of the sea. They're too chewy to eat raw, but excellent for chowder.

This type of creamy, thickened chowder, made with almost any hard-shelled clam, has become known as New England Clam Chowder. But Cape Codders know that quahogs are the only clams to use in clam chowder. And I agree. This is the chowder I always made for the Kennedy clambakes on the beach, just down the bluff from the Big House.

The trick is to add the minimum amount of flour needed to thicken the soup enough so that it clings to a spoon. A good chowder is never heavy or gluey. For contrasting texture, pass a basket of crisp oyster crackers or soda crackers on the side, for guests to crumble into their soup.

2 dozen quahogs
6 ounces meaty salt pork
2 large red or Yukon gold potatoes, peeled and cut into ½-inch dice
1 large onion, diced
⅓ cup all-purpose flour
1 cup half-and-half or light cream
Salt and white pepper
1½ to 2 tablespoons butter
Chopped parsley, for garnish

1. SCRUB THE OUTSIDES of the clams well and rinse in cold water. In a large heavy stockpot, bring 4 quarts of water to a boil. Add the clams, cover, and boil until they open, about 35 minutes.

2. STRAIN THROUGH A COLANDER set over a large heatproof bowl or another pot to catch the clam cooking liquid. Strain this cooking liquid through a sieve lined with several thicknesses of cheesecloth to remove any sand or grit. Boil to reduce by about a third. Measure out and reserve 8 cups of the clam broth.

3. RINSE THE CLAMS under cold running water until they are cool enough to handle. Remove the clams from their shells, rinsing them briefly to wash off any grit. Coarsely chop the clams or cut into ¼-inch dice. Cover and refrigerate while you finish the chowder base.

4. RINSE THE SALT PORK to remove excess salt; pat dry. Cut off the rind. Finely dice the salt pork.

5. IN A MEDIUM SAUCEPAN, boil the diced potatoes in salted water to cover until they are just tender, 8 to 10 minutes. Drain, rinse briefly under cool water, and set aside.

6. IN A LARGE SOUP POT or flameproof casserole, cook the salt pork over medium-low heat until it begins to render its fat, about 5 minutes. Add the onion, raise the heat slightly, and continue to cook until the onion is softened and just beginning to turn golden, 5 to 7 minutes longer.

7. SPRINKLE THE FLOUR over the onion and salt pork and cook, stirring constantly for 1 to 2 minutes without browning. Pour in the reserved 8 cups clam liquid and the half-and-half and bring to a boil, stirring until thickened and smooth. Season with salt and white pepper to taste, keeping in mind the clams and their juices are very salty.

8. ADD THE DICED CLAMS and potatoes to the soup base and immediately remove from the heat. If the clams cook any further, they will be tough; as it is, quahogs are always chewy. Ladle into bowls or large mugs, top each serving with a pat of butter and a dusting of chopped parsley, and serve the chowder piping hot.

My clam chowder was always a hit at the boat lunches, which were frequently hosted by Senator Kennedy, shown here with Eunice Shriver (center) and his wife, the former Victoria Reggie.

Hyannis Port Fish Chowder

SERVES 4 TO 6

WHEN I WAS COOKING AT THE COMPOUND, fishermen would pull up to the docks with their catches early in the morning. They knew I was picky and would take only the freshest of their catch, from which I made this chowder. Under less idyllic circumstances, cod is an excellent choice for this soup; it's clean tasting, surprisingly mild, and meaty in texture. If you can, look for wild, line-caught cod, which many supermarkets carry when available. Since the recipe is so simple, quality is especially important here.

Chunky and light, this savory chowder will feed four to six people as a starter, three or four as a luncheon dish or light supper. If you offer it as a main course, accompany it with one of the interesting salads you'll find on pages 158 to 181. As with my clam chowder, I always serve oyster crackers with fish chowder.

1 medium onion, chopped

3 tablespoons butter, plus more for serving

1½ tablespoons all-purpose flour

2 cups Fish Stock (recipe follows) or substitute 1 cup clam juice diluted with 1 cup water

1 large Yukon gold or red potato, peeled and cut into ½-inch dice

1 pound skinless cod fillet

2 cups milk

Salt and freshly ground pepper

Chopped parsley

1. IN A LARGE SAUCEPAN or soup pot, cook the onion in the butter over medium heat, stirring occasionally, until it is softened and translucent, 3 to 5 minutes. Sprinkle on the flour and cook, stirring, for 1 to 2 minutes without allowing the flour to brown.

2. GRADUALLY STIR IN THE STOCK and bring to a boil, whisking until slightly thickened. Add the diced potato and continue to cook until it is just tender, 5 to 7 minutes.

3. ADD THE WHOLE COD FILLET; this helps prevent the fish from overcooking. Cover, reduce the heat to low, and simmer for 5 minutes. Add the milk and return to a simmer, breaking up the cod into medium-sized chunks with a fork or large spoon. Immediately remove from the heat.

4. SEASON THE CHOWDER with salt and pepper to taste. Serve in soup plates with a sprinkling of chopped parsley and a pat of butter in each bowl.

Fish Stock

MAKES ABOUT 2 QUARTS; 8 CUPS

A CALL AHEAD TO YOUR LOCAL FISH MARKET will usually yield all the bones you need for this stock at no cost. Just be sure to ask for bones from white-fleshed fish: no salmon, which would be too strong.

Unlike with meat stocks, fish bones should not be simmered for longer than half an hour, or the stock can turn bitter.

3 pounds fish bones

3 tablespoons butter

1 medium onion, coarsely chopped

2 celery ribs, coarsely chopped

1 medium leek (white and tender green), well rinsed and coarsely chopped

1 medium carrot, peeled and coarsely chopped

1 cup dry white wine

2 sprigs of parsley

1 bay leaf

½ teaspoon peppercorns

1. RINSE THE FISH BONES well and hack them into 2-inch pieces with a cleaver. Or you can ask your fishmonger to do this.

2. IN A STOCKPOT, melt the butter over medium-low heat. Add the onion, celery, leek, and carrot, cover, and cook until the vegetables are softened but not browned, 5 to 7 minutes.

3. POUR IN THE WINE and bring to a boil. Add 3 quarts of cold water, the parsley sprigs, bay leaf, and peppercorns. Bring to a boil, reduce the heat, and simmer for 25 to 30 minutes.

4. STRAIN THE STOCK through a fine-mesh sieve into a large bowl. Cool quickly by placing the bowl in a larger container of ice and water. Then cover and refrigerate or freeze until you are ready to use the stock.

MY MORNING WITH JACKIE

The weather was perfect—a gorgeous July day that every bride would wish for and that no one deserved more than Caroline Kennedy. All week, I'd been extra-busy, cooking meals for the many family members who had descended on the Compound to begin celebrating Caroline's nuptials to artist and designer Edwin Schlossberg. There were breakfasts, boat lunches for the Senator and his guests, and a parade of elaborate dinners, all leading up to the big day. The wedding was catered by a firm from New York, so I didn't have that extraordinary responsibility, but as the family's personal chef, I was on hand to help the mother of the bride with all matters relating to food and drink—and, as you might imagine, there were many!

That morning, I accompanied Jackie on foot as she crisscrossed the grounds of the compound, making last-minute arrangements to ensure the day would go smoothly—for everyone, not just her family and friends. She hadn't begun dressing for the wedding yet; her signature dark hair was covered almost completely by the type of kerchief she usually sported in the wind off the ocean, and she wore no make-up. Still, she was beautiful. By then, I was comfortable with her and felt we had a congenial and respectful working relationship. I sometimes called her Mrs. Onassis and other times just "Jackie."

What struck me was her enormous attention to detail as well as her compassion, which was a quiet but deep part of her nature. Even on the day of her own daughter's wedding, Jackie voiced concern for the welfare of the many people working on the event, from police to kitchen workers and servers. She wanted to make sure they had a place to take a break during those times when their services were not needed, somewhere they could relax, sit down, and get a bite to eat.

"I accompanied Jackie…as she crisscrossed the grounds of the Compound,

That morning, as we sauntered from the tent set up next to her house to the street where the police were assembling to handle traffic and maintain the family's privacy, she seemed calm and reflective, though I knew she had a lot of details on her mind. She had just finished telling a police officer where he and his men could get coffee and a sandwich later in the day, and we had turned to head back toward the yard near Rose's house, where hundreds of folding chairs would soon be set up.

making last-minute arrangements to ensure the day would go smoothly."

"It's hard for me to come here," she said quietly. "There are so many memories."

I was touched and taken aback at being taken into her confidence. She was always warm and pleasant to me but kept the distance that I expected about her private thoughts. But her daughter's wedding had to have been a milestone that put her in touch with her deepest feelings—and made them hard to keep in. With her revealing remark, my own memories of the Compound came flooding back, images etched in all of our minds of John and Jackie Kennedy as newlyweds, sailing a Sunfish, frolicking in the water; of little Caroline and John-John on the beach; of the President rocking in his famous chair on the porch of their nearby home. Jackie's return to the Compound as a young widow with two small children must have been excruciating. In my years at the compound, I had often seen her visiting her mother-in-law, Rose, sometimes with her grown children, other times, alone. She usually made it a day trip and left without spending the night, going on to her own house on Martha's Vineyard. I often wondered why she was so quick to depart. Now I understood.

A moment later, she was back on the job, busy arranging that picture-perfect day. I worked especially hard in the hours that followed to make sure her remembrance of Caroline's wedding would be perfect and filled with joy, a happy memory to overlay some of the sadder ones of the past. I like to think that's how it turned out for her.

FACING PAGE: *Jackie conferring with Neil the morning of Caroline's wedding in July of 1986.*
TOP: *Jackie regularly visited Rose, coming and going from her house in Martha's Vineyard, sometimes aboard her companion Maurice Templeton's yacht.*

Lobster Bisque

SERVES 6 TO 8

THE SENATOR HAD A LICENSE FOR LOBSTER TRAPS, which we used to keep in Hyannis Port Harbor. We would check them daily. When there wasn't an abundance of lobster, which was quite often, I would always make a bisque out of the few that we caught or from any culls—lobsters missing a claw. Since lobster bisque is labor intensive, if there were enough, I'd make a double batch and freeze the extra. I prefer basmati rice in this recipe for its nutty flavor.

8 cups Lobster Stock (recipe follows)

½ cup basmati rice

1 cup light cream or half-and-half

1½ tablespoons butter

1 cup finely diced cooked lobster meat (reserved from Lobster Stock, which follows)

2 tablespoons dry sherry

1 tablespoon Cognac or brandy

1. IN A LARGE SAUCEPAN, bring 4 cups of the lobster stock to a boil. Add the rice and cook until it is very soft, 15 to 20 minutes. Remove from the heat and let cool slightly, then puree in a blender or food processor until very smooth.

2. IN THE SAME SAUCEPAN, bring the remaining 4 cups lobster stock to a boil. Stir in the pureed rice mixture and the cream, reduce the heat to low, and simmer for 10 minutes.

3. MEANWHILE, MELT THE BUTTER in a heavy medium skillet. Add the lobster meat and sauté until hot, about 1 minute. Add the sherry and Cognac and cook, tossing, for another minute. Remove from the heat.

4. TO SERVE, LADLE THE LOBSTER BISQUE into 6 to 8 soup plates and spoon a bit of the lobster meat onto each serving.

Lobster Stock

MAKES ABOUT 8 CUPS

CULL LOBSTERS ARE SPECIMENS that are not perfect enough to serve whole. It won't matter a bit to the taste of this rich stock, and sometimes you can get them at a bargain price.

2 live cull lobsters (about 1 pound each)
3 sprigs of fresh parsley
1½ teaspoons tarragon, preferably fresh
1 teaspoon thyme leaves, preferably fresh
1 bay leaf
1½ teaspoons whole black peppercorns
2 tablespoons extra virgin olive oil
1 medium onion, chopped
1 celery rib, coarsely chopped
1 small carrot, peeled and thickly sliced
1 garlic clove, chopped
2 tablespoons Cognac or brandy
2 tablespoons dry white wine
¾ cup tomato puree

1. WITH A HEAVY CLEAVER, chop up the lobsters in their shells into 2-inch chunks. You may want to ask your fishmonger to do this for you. Tie the parsley, tarragon, thyme, bay leaf, and peppercorns in a double thickness of cheesecloth.

2. IN A SMALL STOCKPOT or large flameproof casserole, heat the olive oil over medium-high heat. Add the lobster chunks and cook, tossing, until the shells start to turn red, about 2 minutes. Add the onion, celery, carrot, and garlic. Sauté until the vegetables are slightly softened, about 3 minutes longer. Then add the Cognac and white wine and let them bubble up.

3. ADD THE CHEESECLOTH BAG of herbs, the tomato puree and 2½ quarts (10 cups) of water. Bring to a boil. After about 15 minutes, remove the lobster pieces; turn off the heat, but leave the stock in the pot. As soon as the lobster is cool enough to handle, remove the meat from the shells; reserve the shells. Refrigerate the lobster meat for the bisque (above) or any other use you like.

4. RETURN THE SHELLS to the pot and simmer the stock, partially covered, for about 30 minutes longer, or until the flavor is rich. At this point remove from the stove and strain the stock. (If you have a china cap with small holes, pound the shells and vegetables to extract as much extra juices as possible and add them to the stock.)

5. RETURN THE STOCK to the pot and boil until the flavor is intense, about 5 minutes. Let cool, then strain again through a fine mesh sieve, cover, and refrigerate until ready to use. (The stock will keep well in the refrigerator for up 2 days or in the freezer for up to 2 months.)

Lobster Stew

SERVES 4

QUICK AND ELEGANT AT THE SAME TIME, this rich stew served as both a starter at dinner and a one-dish meal at lunch at the Compound, accompanied simply with crusty French bread. Note, there's only about ½ cup liquid per person; all the emphasis is on the succulent lobster.

¼ cup finely chopped onion
4 tablespoons butter
1 to 1⅓ pounds cooked lobster meat , cut into ½-inch chunks
¼ cup sherry wine, preferably medium-dry (amontillado)
¼ cup lobster stock (optional but desirable)
1¼ cups light cream or half-and-half
¼ teaspoon paprika
Salt and freshly ground pepper
4 teaspoons minced fresh chives

1. IN A MEDIUM-SIZE DEEP SKILLET or heavy saucepan, cook the onion in the butter over medium heat until softened and translucent, about 3 minutes.

2. ADD THE COOKED LOBSTER MEAT and toss to coat with the butter. Pour in the sherry and bring to a boil. Add the lobster stock, if you have it, and boil until the liquid is reduced by half.

3. ADD THE LIGHT CREAM AND PAPRIKA. Season with salt and pepper to taste. Bring just to a boil. Immediately ladle into soup plates and garnish with the chives. Serve at once.

Oyster Stew

4 SERVINGS AS A FIRST COURSE OR 2 AS A MAIN COURSE

It's a Cape Cod maxim: the best oyster stew is the simplest oyster stew. Of course, it goes without saying that when a recipe has this few ingredients, they must be of the highest quality.

Be sure to shuck the oysters over a bowl to catch all their juices, or liquor. Freezing them for 15 minutes before you begin makes prying open their shells much easier. If you have your fishmonger shuck them for you, be sure to tell him you need ½ cup oyster liquor.

4 tablespoons butter
1 small onion, finely chopped
32 freshly shucked oysters, such as Cotuits, liquor reserved
4 cups milk, warmed
Salt and freshly ground pepper
Chopped parsley
Oyster crackers

1. IN A LARGE WIDE SKILLET, melt the butter over medium heat. Add the onion and cook, stirring occasionally, until it is softened and translucent, about 5 minutes.

2. ADD THE RAW OYSTERS with their liquor and the warmed milk. Season with salt and pepper to taste. Heat just until bubbles begin to form around the edge of the pan, 2 to 3 minutes.

3. IMMEDIATELY REMOVE FROM THE HEAT and ladle into bowls, dividing the oysters evenly. Garnish with a pinch of chopped parsley and pass a basket of oyster crackers on the side.

Herbed Mushroom Soup

SERVES 6

I LIKE TEXTURE IN MANY OF MY SOUPS. That's why the mushrooms here are chopped, but the soup is not pureed. Serve in cream soup bowls if you have them and garnish with chopped parsley or more of the basil or thyme.

3 tablespoons butter or olive oil
1 medium onion, chopped
1 pound mushrooms, finely diced
3 tablespoons all-purpose flour
⅓ cup medium-dry sherry
6 cups chicken stock
1 teaspoon chopped fresh basil
1 teaspoon fresh or dried thyme leaves
⅓ cup heavy cream
Salt and freshly ground pepper

1. IN A LARGE SAUCEPAN, melt the butter over medium-high heat. Add the onion and cook, stirring occasionally, until just softened, about 3 minutes. Add the mushrooms and continue to cook, stirring from time to time until they give up their liquid but are not browned, 5 to 7 minutes.

2. SPRINKLE THE FLOUR over the mushrooms and onion and cook, stirring for about 2 minutes. Add the sherry and bring to a boil. Whisk in the chicken stock and return to a boil, stirring until the liquid is slightly thickened.

3. REDUCE THE HEAT to medium-low; add the cream and thyme. Simmer for 10 minutes. Season with salt and pepper to taste.

Chef's Note: To clean the mushrooms for this dish, simply rinse them quickly under cold running water, drain in a colander, and pat them dry with paper towels.

NO SWIMMING
"On the nights when the moon was full, the Kennedy clambakes
had a special luminescent quality, as though the beach were a
Hollywood stage set lit by a master technician."

Fish *and* Shellfish

Hyannis Port Yacht Club dock at dusk

Grilled Striped Bass with Avocado Relish

SERVES 4

QUICK AND LIGHT, THIS IS AN IDEAL SUMMERTIME DISH. The cool relish topping is a colorful guacamole-like version of fresh salsa, with the addition of cucumber, which I like with fish. A touch of balsamic vinegar adds a deeper note. While the fish in point here is striped bass, which ran in huge schools off the Cape when we lived there, you could serve this relish with any grilled fish; adjust your cooking time depending upon texture and thickness.

Avocado Relish (recipe follows)
4 striped bass fillets, 6 to 7 ounces each
3 tablespoons extra virgin olive oil
Salt and freshly ground pepper

1. PREPARE THE AVOCADO RELISH ahead of time, because you'll want to serve it as soon as the fish is cooked.

2. LIGHT A HOT FIRE in a barbecue grill using hardwood charcoal, banking the coals on one side. Or preheat your gas grill to high.

3. BRUSH BOTH SIDES of the striped bass with 1 tablespoon of the olive oil. Season lightly with salt and pepper. Place in an oiled fish grilling rack, if you have one.

4. SET THE FISH FILLETS over the hot fire and grill, turning the fillets carefully, for 3 to 4 minutes a side, until lightly browned.

5. SHIFT THE FISH over to the cooler side of the grill or reduce the heat on the gas grill to low. Cook for 3 minutes. Again, carefully turn the fish over and continue to cook for 2 to 4 minutes longer.

6. TRANSFER THE FISH TO PLATES. Top each fillet with a spoonful of the Avocado Relish. Pass the remainder on the side.

Chef's Note: "Striper" has been one of the most prized fish along the coast of New England since Colonial times. Huge schools of striped bass used to run close to shore, but because their stocks declined so greatly in recent years, the Division of Marine Fisheries has put a limit on the number of fish that can be caught between May and November. So when you see wild striped bass in your fish market, get some because it won't last long.

Avocado Relish

MAKES ABOUT 3 CUPS

WHILE I SUGGEST THIS AS AN ACCOMPANIMENT to fish, it works equally well with marinated grilled beef and can even be offered as a dip with tortilla chips. You can make the relish in advance and refrigerate it, or prepare it while the fish is grilling. Either way, the balsamic vinegar will help the avocado to retain its color.

1 avocado, cut into ⅜-inch dice
1 small red onion, finely diced
1 tablespoon balsamic vinegar
½ teaspoon sea salt
1 beefsteak tomato, peeled, seeded, and cut into ⅜-inch dice
½ cup cucumber, peeled, seeded, and cut into ⅜-inch dice
1 tablespoon minced fresh chives
1 tablespoon finely chopped fresh basil
2 tablespoons extra virgin olive oil

1. PUT THE DICED AVOCADO and red onion into a bowl. Add the balsamic vinegar and sea salt and toss gently to mix.

2. ADD THE TOMATO, cucumber, chives, basil, and olive oil. Toss again gently to mix. Cover and refrigerate for up to 3 hours before serving.

Cape Cod Baked Haddock with Mornay Sauce

SERVES 4

MRS. EUNICE SHRIVER, MARIA'S MOTHER, loved this traditional dish. I usually served it with boiled potatoes and buttered broccoli. For a lighter everyday meal, you could skip the sauce and present the baked fish plain, with lemon wedges.

1⅓ to 1½ pounds haddock fillet
½ cup fresh bread crumbs
½ cup Ritz Cracker crumbs
1 stick (4 ounces) butter, melted
¼ cup dry sherry
Lemon wedges or Mornay Sauce (recipe follows)

1. PREHEAT THE OVEN to 400 degrees F. Cut the fish into 4 equal pieces.

2. IN A WIDE SHALLOW BOWL or pie plate, toss together the bread crumbs and cracker crumbs. Add the melted butter and sherry and mix with a fork until well blended.

3. DREDGE THE HADDOCK FILLETS in the buttered crumbs, patting lightly to help the coating adhere. Make sure the fillets are well covered with crumbs. Arrange the fish in an oiled baking pan large enough to hold the pieces in a single layer without crowding.

4. BAKE FOR 15 MINUTES, or until the coating is crisp and the fish is just opaque in the center but still moist. Do not overcook. Serve hot with lemon wedges or with the cheese sauce that follows.

Mornay Sauce

MAKES ABOUT 1¾ CUPS

2 tablespoons butter
1½ tablespoons all-purpose flour
1½ cups half-and-half or milk
½ cup shredded mild white Cheddar cheese
Splash each of Tabasco and Worcestershire sauce
Salt and freshly ground pepper

1. IN A HEAVY MEDIUM SAUCEPAN, melt the butter over medium-low heat. Add the flour and cook, stirring, for 1 to 2 minutes to make a roux. Whisk in the half-and-half or milk and bring to a boil, whisking constantly. Reduce the heat to low and simmer, whisking, for 2 to 3 minutes longer.

2. REMOVE FROM THE HEAT and add the shredded cheese. Whisk until smooth. Whisk in the Tabasco and Worcestershire sauce. Season with salt and pepper to taste.

Mediterranean-Style Halibut with Clams and Mussels

SERVES 4

COLORFUL AND EXTREMELY FLAVORFUL, this dish is a seafood feast in a bowl. Serve with garlic bread and sautéed zucchini on the side.

1⅓ to 1½ pounds halibut fillets, skinned

4 tablespoons olive oil

1 tablespoon minced shallot

2 garlic cloves, finely chopped

¼ cup dry white wine

1 tablespoon Pernod or anisette

16 littleneck clams, cleaned

16 mussels, cleaned

4 cups hot fish broth or 2 cups clam broth and 2 cups reduced-sodium chicken stock

½ cup marinara sauce or tomato sauce

½ teaspoon dried oregano

2 tablespoons chopped parsley

1. PREHEAT THE OVEN TO 375 DEGREES F. Cut the fish into 4 equal pieces. Heat 2 tablespoons of the olive oil in a very large cast-iron skillet over medium-high heat. Arrange the halibut fillets in the pan without crowding and sauté, turning once, until browned, about 2 to 3 minutes per side.

2. TRANSFER THE HALIBUT to a baking dish and bake for 10 minutes.

3. MEANWHILE, ADD THE SHALLOT and garlic to the same skillet you cooked the fish in and cook over medium heat for 1 to 2 minutes to soften. Add the wine and Pernod and scrape up any brown bits from the bottom of the pan. Add the clams and mussels, cover tightly, and steam for 5 to 7 minutes, until the shellfish open. Discard any clams or mussels that remain tightly closed.

4. POUR IN THE FISH STOCK, marinara or tomato sauce, oregano, and half the parsley. Cover and simmer for 2 to 3 minutes.

5. WHEN THE BROTH IS HOT, transfer the shellfish to soup places and place the halibut on top. Ladle the broth over all and garnish with the remaining parsley.

Chef's Note: Some chef's techniques are not very appropriate for the home kitchen. However, everyone who tries our professional way of cooking thicker fish by searing it first on top of the stove and finishing it in the oven agrees it's superior and in some ways easier, because you can control the final cooking.

Citrus-Glazed Grilled Salmon

SERVES 4

I SERVED THIS ATTRACTIVE DISH OFTEN at the Kennedys' during the summer months. In fact, it was the main course at the luncheon for Rose's 100th birthday. The whole family was there, including Jackie, John, and Caroline, who always paid their respects. A telegram even arrived from Pope John Paul II, which thrilled Rose.

The secret to cooking fish is very simple: Don't overcook it. I always served this gorgeous salmon with a vegetable couscous salad and some baby salad greens.

1½ to 2 pounds center-cut salmon fillets, skinned
2 tablespoons butter
1 orange, cut into 8 slices
½ cup freshly squeezed orange juice
1 tablespoon balsamic vinegar
1 tablespoon finely chopped pickled ginger
¼ cup sugar
3 tablespoons Grand Marnier

1. LIGHT A HOT FIRE in a barbecue grill or set your gas grill to hot. At the same time, preheat your oven to 375 degrees F. Cut the salmon fillets into 4 equal pieces.

2. MAKE THE CITRUS GLAZE. In a large nonreactive ovenproof skillet, melt the butter over medium-high heat. Add the orange slices and brown lightly on both sides, about 1 minute per side. Add the orange juice, balsamic vinegar, pickled ginger, and sugar. Bring to a boil, stirring to dissolve the sugar. Boil for 3 to 4 minutes to reduce to a syrup thick enough to coat the back of a spoon. Remove from the heat and stir in the Grand Marnier. Set the citrus glaze aside in the pan.

3. WHEN FIRE IS HOT, sear the salmon fillets meaty side down for 3 to 4 minutes, until nicely browned with grill marks.

4. TRANSFER THE SALMON fillets skinned side down to the skillet holding the citus glaze and baste to coat. Place in the oven and bake for 7 to 8 minutes, or until cooked through but still moist. Serve with the remaining glaze drizzled over the fish. Garnish with the orange slices.

Chef's Note: There are many varieties of salmon; some are better than others, but all offer very good eating. While farmed salmon is acceptable, wild is a real treat. Most comes from the Pacific, where varieties include Coho; Chinook, or king, salmon, which is the largest of any salmon; and Copper River salmon and sockeye salmon, both of which are leaner and exceptionally dark in color.

Poached Salmon Fillets with Dilled Egg Sauce

SERVES 6

THE OLD-FASHIONED CREAMY EGG SAUCE served here was one of Jackie's favorites. We often served it over poached salmon for Sunday lunch. I usually accompanied the fish with basmati rice, fresh spring peas, sliced cucumbers, and garden-ripe tomatoes when they were in season.

2 to 2½ pounds center-cut salmon fillet, at least ¾ inch thick, skinned
1½ quarts Court Bouillon (recipe follows)
1 cup heavy cream
2 hard-boiled eggs, finely diced
1 tablespoon chopped fresh dill weed
Pinch of grated nutmeg
Salt and freshly ground pepper

1. CUT THE SALMON INTO 6 EQUAL PIECES. Bring the court bouillon to a boil in a 12-inch skillet or large flameproof casserole. Reduce the heat to medium-low and add the salmon. If for any reason the bouillon does not cover the fish, add some water or white wine. Simmer the fish for about 12 minutes, or until the salmon is just barely translucent in the center. (The fish will continue cooking after you remove it.)

2. WHILE THE SALMON IS POACHING, make the sauce: In a medium saucepan boil the cream until it is reduced to ¾ cup, 3 to 5 minutes. (You'll need a larger saucepan than you'd expect because the cream bubbles up.)

3. STIR IN THE DICED HARD-BOILED EGGS and fresh dill. Season with the nutmeg and salt and pepper to taste. Keep the sauce warm.

4. WHEN THE SALMON IS DONE, carefully remove each piece with a wide slotted spatula and arrange on a platter or individual plates. Spoon the egg sauce on top and serve at once.

Court Bouillon

MAKES ABOUT 1½ QUARTS

1 large onion, quartered
2 medium carrots, thickly sliced
4 sprigs of parsley
3 sprigs of fresh thyme or ½ teaspoon dried
1 bay leaf
2 cups dry white wine
1 teaspoon whole black peppercorns
Salt

1. PUT THE ONION, carrots, parsley, thyme, bay leaf, and wine in a pot. Add 6 cups of water. Bring to a boil, reduce the heat slightly and simmer, partially covered, for 30 minutes.

2. ADD THE PEPPERCORNS and simmer for 10 minutes longer. Strain through a sieve. Season with salt to taste, and the court bouillon is ready to use for poaching seafood or vegetables.

Sautéed Lemon Sole

SERVES 4

AT THE CAPE, WE ATE THE FRESHEST FISH AVAILABLE. One kind I always knew I could get was excellent flat fish: sole or flounder. Sole is a tad more delicate than flounder, but they are both exceedingly mild, white-fleshed fish that almost everyone enjoys. Serve this simple dish with rice and Peas Française (page 143) or your favorite green vegetable.

4 lemon sole fillets, 4 to 5 ounces each, or substitute grey sole or flounder
4 eggs
½ cup dry white wine
¼ cup all-purpose flour
Salt and freshly ground pepper
2 tablespoons vegetable oil
1 tablespoon butter
1 teaspoon minced shallot
Juice of 1 lemon
2 teaspoons chopped parsley

1. PAT THE FISH FILLETS dry with paper towels.

2. IN A WIDE SHALLOW BOWL, whisk the eggs together with ¼ cup of the white wine to make an egg wash.

3. IN ANOTHER SHALLOW BOWL, mix the flour with ¼ teaspoon salt and ⅛ teaspoon pepper. Dredge the fish fillets in the seasoned flour to coat both sides; gently shake any excess back into the bowl. Dip the sole fillets in the egg wash and let them soak for up to 30 minutes until you are ready to sauté them.

4. HEAT A SAUTÉ PAN or large skillet over medium-high heat. Add the oil and heat until hot but not smoking. With your fingers or tongs, one by one lift the sole fillets, letting excess egg wash drip back into the bowl and add to the hot oil in the pan. Sauté, carefully turning once with a wide spatula, until golden brown, 3 to 4 minutes per side. Remove to a platter.

5. POUR OUT ANY OIL that remains in the skillet. Add the butter and shallot and cook over medium heat for about 2 minutes to soften the shallot. Pour in the remaining ¼ cup wine and boil, scraping up any brown bits from the bottom of the pan with a wooden spoon or spatula, for about 1 minute. Add the lemon juice and parsley and pour over the fish. Serve at once.

CAROLINE'S FAIRY TALE WEDDING

Caroline Kennedy, the first baby born in the White House in over 50 years, had fame thrust upon her from the moment she opened her eyes. As we watched her grow from an infant to a beautiful toddler, we fell in love with her as naturally as her parents did. Are there any more cherished photographs in our history than those of Caroline with her father, leading her on her pony Macaroni up the White House walkway or hiding impishly under the President's desk in the Oval Office?

Under any circumstances, we would have always been drawn to those images. Because of all Caroline has lost since then, we see these pictures now through a poignant film of protectiveness and sorrow. Like her brother, John, Caroline has always been beloved—by everyone, it seems—because of her grace and generosity in the face of so much grief.

In 1986, when she announced plans to marry artist Edwin Schlossberg that summer, the public and media reaction matched the level of the country's affection for her. Her marriage would be the heart of her most intimate life, but her wedding would be a grand event, attended by world leaders, celebrities, media stars, and hundreds of members of the royal family—the Kennedys, that is. It would be closed to the press, but that would not stop every news group in the world from showing up in Hyannis Port and trying to get a piece of the action. As in so many areas of her life, here, too, Caroline straddled her public and private roles with style and warmth.

She and Ed chose July 19th, his birthday, to be wed at Our Lady of Victory in Centerville, a few miles from Hyannis and the family compound, for her reception. Designer Caroline Herrera designed her white silk organza gown. It had a round neck, short sleeves, and a plain skirt that gathered into a long train. It was dotted with embroidered shamrocks, in honor of her Irish heritage. Her beloved Uncle Teddy, her father's only surviving brother, had the honor of walking her down the aisle. John Jr. was the best man, and Maria Shriver, who had married Arnold Schwarzenegger three months before, the matron of honor. The night before, at the rehearsal dinner, John had touched everyone when he said to his new brother-

"Her marriage would be the heart of her most intimate

but her wedding would be a grand event…"

in-law, "All our lives, it's just been the three of us, Mommy, Caroline, and me. Now there are four." The wedding guest list was far larger, close to 500 people. They included many of her father's White House associates and cabinet members, her aunt Lee Radziwill, artists Jasper Johns and Robert Rauschenberg, Carly Simon, who sang "Chapel of Love" and "Loving You's the Right Thing to Do" at the reception, and writer-editor George Plimpton, who put on a fireworks display over the water when the sun went down.

That day, Caroline was our fairy tale bride, her brother was our favorite best man, and her mother Jackie was once again our beloved First Lady.

FACING PAGE: *Maria Shriver adjusting the hem of Caroline Kennedy Schlossberg's dress outside the church just after the wedding service.*
ABOVE: *Caroline Kennedy and husband Edwin Schlossberg in front of the church just after their wedding on July 19, 1986.*

Grilled Swordfish with Tomato-Basil Butter

SERVES 4

I MUST CONFESS, UP AT THE COMPOUND, we had so much fish coming in fresh off the boats, I'd serve one person a 10-ounce steak, just like prime rib, spilling over the plate. These days, a 6-ounce portion is more than respectable, especially when paired with Chive Rice Cakes (page 156), which I like with this dish, and a nice green vegetable like asparagus or baby green beans.

2 swordfish steaks, cut 1 inch thick (10 to 12 ounces each)
2 tablespoons extra virgin olive oil
1 tablespoon fresh lemon juice
1 garlic clove, smashed
Salt and freshly ground pepper
4 tablespoons Tomato-Basil Butter (recipe follows)

1. MARINATE THE SWORDFISH in the olive oil seasoned with the lemon juice, garlic, ¼ teaspoon salt and ⅛ teaspoon pepper for 20 to 30 minutes at room temperature, or for up to 1 hour in the refrigerator.

2. MEANWHILE, PREPARE A HOT FIRE in a charcoal grill with the coals banked to one side. Or preheat a gas grill set to high.

3. PLACE THE SWORDFISH STEAKS on the hot side of the grill and cook for about 3 minutes. Then turn the fish over with a wide spatula and cook for about another 3 minutes.

4. MOVE THE SWORDFISH to the cooler side of the grill—or reduce the heat on the gas grill to medium-low—and cook for 3 to 4 minutes longer. You want the fish to be white in the center but still nice and juicy. Remember, the fish will keep cooking after you remove it from the grill, and the last thing you want is to do is overcook it.

5. QUICKLY TRANSFER to a cutting board, divide the steaks in half, and put each piece on a large plate. Top the swordfish steaks with a medallion of Tomato-Basil Butter. The butter will melt into the hot fish. Serve at once.

Chef's Note: Whenever I grill, I prefer using hardwood charcoal, such as mesquite, hickory, cherry, or apple, which is available in most grocery stores. It results in a much hotter flame than you get from a standard outdoor gas grill and then, of course, there's that lovely kiss of smoke.

Tomato Basil Butter

MAKES ABOUT ½ CUP

CHEFS LOVE WHAT WE CALL "COMPOUND BUTTERS" like this one. They offer a great way to impart a lot of flavor simply without a sauce, and they can be made well in advance and refrigerated. This particular one is good on all fish, shrimp, and vegetables.

1 stick (4 ounces) butter, slightly softened
2 tablespoons dry white wine
2 tablespoons tomato sauce
1½ teaspoons minced shallot
1½ teaspoons chopped fresh basil
1 garlic clove, crushed through a press

1. IN A BOWL with a wooden spoon, blend together the butter, wine, tomato sauce, shallot, basil, and garlic until thoroughly mixed.

2. TURN THE FLAVORED BUTTER out onto a sheet of waxed paper and roll into a log. Wrap tightly and refrigerate until chilled and set. Cut off rounds as needed. Any extra can be frozen for up to 2 months.

CLAMBAKES ON OLD CAPE COD

On nights when the moon was full, the Kennedy clambakes had a special luminescent quality, as though the beach were a Hollywood stage set lit by a master technician. But even when the moon was just a brilliant sliver in the distant sapphire sky, these were very special occasions—and they happened four or five times every summer.

Clambakes for 125 to 150 people—the usual guest list—were the Senator's favorite way of entertaining, and his enthusiasm was contagious. Gathered on the sandy beach at sunset would be Jackie Onassis and her children, Maria Shriver and Arnold Schwarzenegger, dozens of politicians, and celebrities who might have sailed over from Nantucket and Martha's Vineyard. The only family members not present were the very youngest children.

"It was the dazzling pink and purple sunsets, the starry skies,

I was always happy to take credit for the menu and the presentation, but it was the dazzling pink and purple sunsets, the starry skies, and the smells of the sea and seafood steaming to perfection that made the evenings so memorable. Being on Cape Cod and the beach just as the sun was going down. The smell from the bake with the steamed clams, lobsters, and corn on the cob, and the chowder cooking on a portable burner, acted like a magnet. We would set the tent about 10 feet from the high tide mark on the beach. Each table would have a ship's lantern on it. The bake itself would be about 15 feet from the tent. I would set torches around the bake and the beach. And, of course, there was always a bonfire at the end of the night for the marshmallows, and every once in a while the band would play the song Patti Page made famous, "Old Cape Cod."

For the guests, the festivities began when they arrived just before sunset at the Senator's house and walked across the lawn to the dunes and the wooden staircase that led down to the beach. As they descended the stairs, they'd see two tents set up on the beach, a small one for my cooking supplies and a much larger one with tables and chairs where they sat down and ate. The flaps on the larger tent would always be up on all sides, so people could wander easily across the sand, grab a mug of clam chowder while waiting for the main course, and see the extraordinary sights from every angle.

Between the tents was the bake itself, which, unlike traditional clambakes, revolved around the special gigantic pans where the food was cooked. Next to those was a handmade wooden rowboat, made by the Senator's son Ted Jr., which was raised off the ground on a mound of sand. We used the row boat, filled with seaweed, as a "buffet table" for food when it came out of the bake pan. As with all the

Littleneck Pan Roast with Linguiça and Pernod

4 SERVINGS

OF COURSE, WHETHER THE KENNEDYS WERE IN Boston, Washington, D.C., or New York, they were used to eating at the best restaurants. So while a shellfish pan roast is traditionally an extremely simple affair—a shellfish stew in one pot—the family always applauded my more sophisticated Mediterranean take. I always serve this dish with thick slabs of garlic bread for sopping up the delicious sauce.

3 dozen littleneck clams
1 medium shallot, minced
2 garlic cloves, minced
⅓ cup extra virgin olive oil
1 cup dry white wine
2 tablespoons Pernod
6 ounces linguiça or grilled hot Italian sausage, thinly sliced
2 cups tomato sauce, preferably Homemade Tomato Sauce (recipe follows)
¼ cup chopped fresh basil
Freshly ground pepper
1 package (10 ounces) prewashed baby spinach

1. SCRUB THE CLAMS well with a coarse brush and soak in a bowl of cold water for about 15 minutes. Lift them into a colander and rinse well; let drain.

2. IN A LARGE FLAMEPROOF CASSEROLE or paella pan, cook the shallot and garlic in the olive oil over medium heat for 1 to 2 minutes to soften without browning. Carefully pour in the wine and Pernod. Bring to a boil. Add the clams, cover, and steam for 3 to 4 minutes, until the clams just start to open.

3. AT THIS POINT, ADD THE LINGUIÇA, tomato sauce, basil, and a few turns of the pepper mill. Bring to a boil, reduce the heat, and simmer until the sausage is heated through, about 5 minutes.

4. ADD THE SPINACH and toss over the heat until just barely wilted, 1 to 2 minutes. Serve immediately in soup plates.

Chef's Note: Linguiça is a fairly spicy Portuguese sausage. If it's not available in your local market, substitute hot Italian.

Homemade Tomato Sauce

MAKES ABOUT 4 CUPS

WHILE THIS SAUCE IS EXTREMELY EASY, it does require an hour or two of your time. Since it tastes significantly better than anything you can buy in a jar. I suggest you make up a double batch and freeze it in half-pint, pint, and even quart containers, so it's on hand whenever you need it.

2 tablespoons butter or extra virgin olive oil
½ cup finely diced salt pork (about 2 ounces)
1 medium onion, chopped
1 carrot, peeled and chopped
1 small celery rib, chopped
2 tablespoons all-purpose flour
1 cup chicken stock
2 garlic cloves, minced
1 can (28 ounces) Italian peeled tomatoes, juices reserved
2 tablespoons chopped fresh basil or parsley
1 teaspoon thyme leaves, preferably fresh
1 bay leaf
1 teaspoon sugar

1. IN A LARGE NONREACTIVE SAUCEPAN, melt the butter or heat the olive oil over medium heat. Add the salt pork and cook for 3 to 4 minutes, until the fat starts to render.

2. ADD THE ONION, CARROT, AND CELERY and cook, stirring occasionally, for 5 minutes. Sprinkle on the flour and cook, stirring, for 1 to 2 minutes without allowing the flour to brown.

3. STIR IN THE STOCK. Bring to a boil, whisking to make a thin paste. Add the garlic, tomatoes and their liquid, basil, thyme, bay leaf, and sugar. Mix well. Bring to a boil, crushing the tomatoes with a large spoon. Reduce the heat to low, partially cover, and simmer for 1 hour.

4. STRAIN THE SAUCE through a mesh sieve, pressing down on the vegetables and salt pork to extract as much liquid as possible. Let cool, then cover and refrigerate for up to 5 days or freeze for up to 4 months before using.

Grilled Lobster

SERVES 4

WHEN PEOPLE THINK OF LOBSTER IN NEW ENGLAND, they usually think of steamed lobsters or broiled stuffed in restaurants. But no technique beats grilling to bring out their sweetness and flavor. This was the Senator's favorite lobster dish.

4 live or freshly killed lobsters, 1½ pounds each
Melted butter
1 whole lemon, cut into wedges

1. HOLDING THE LOBSTER down on its back, use a large sharp knife to cut down the center from stem to stern, cutting only through the soft shell on the belly and part of the meat but not all the way through. Be careful doing this so that the lobster does not slip while you are cutting. Using your hands, now spread the lobster tail and cavity open. Then remove the dark sack at the back of the head and discard.

2. I PREFER USING hardwood charcoal, which is available at most grocery stores, because it is much hotter than most gas grills and imparts more of a smoky taste. Bank your charcoal to one side of the grill so you will be able to move the lobster to regulate the amount of heat while cooking.

3. PLACE THE LOBSTERS on the hot side of the grill on their backs for about 5 minutes. The shells will turn red and then begin to blacken slightly. Move the lobsters to the cooler side of the grill periodically to keep them from charring.

4. TURN THE LOBSTERS over onto their belly and cook for another 5 to 6 minutes. A gas grill may require an extra 2 or 3 minutes.

5. REMOVE THE LOBSTERS from the grill, invert onto plates, and brush the exposed tail meat with some of the melted butter. Serve the remainder in small individual bowls and be sure each person gets 1 or 2 lemon wedges with their lobster.

Chef's Note: If cutting up the lobster as described in Step 1 is a task you can't handle, ask your fish market to prepare the lobsters for you. In that case, be sure to coordinate so they are cut just before you pick them up to cook them; they won't last all day.

LOBSTER FOR THE POT

I always used massive amounts of seafood, especially lobsters, in my cooking at the Compound. Everyone in the family loved them, and it was so typical of the Cape. But seafood has to be impeccably fresh. Lobsters in particular suffer from even a week in a tank. Like the corn on the cob they are often served with in summer, they are sweetest and most succulent when just harvested. My second year working for the Kennedys, the Senator came up with an idea.

"Neil," he said to me one afternoon, "why don't we get some lobster traps for the harbor?" This involved a bit more than meets the eye. Kennedy's colors. (Each lobster fishermen has a distinct marking for their buoys so they are recognized by other fishermen.) The next day, we took the speedboat out into the harbor, placed the traps in water near the jetty, about twenty feet apart, and baited them with mackerel. The Styrofoam buoys tied to each cage with a nylon rope bobbed on the surface of the water.

Sometimes we'd check the traps first thing in the morning. I got pretty good at pulling them live out of the cages with no gloves on! They'd go directly into a five-gallon plastic bucket, which I'd cart up to

"Sometimes we got seven, eight, or even ten lobsters a day; other times, nothing."

To protect the beds, lobster fishing is closely regulated in Massachusetts. We had to go to the Hyannis Town Hall and obtain the licenses needed for twelve traps, the maximum each household was allowed. Next we went to the marine supply store and bought the traps and buoys along with yards and yards of line to secure the pots to the bottom of the harbor.

With twelve metal cages in hand, we returned to Hyannis Port, and I painted all the buoys blue and white: Senator

the house. Other times, after a day of sailing or to amuse the children, the Senator would see if we'd caught any lobsters. Sometimes we got seven, eight, or even ten lobsters a day; other times, nothing. When we were lucky, I'd often boil a lobster or two right away for salads and keep the rest in the refrigerator until it was time to grill them or to make lobster stew or lobster bisque. My Lobster Salad with Fresh Fruit (page 175) was a perennial favorite, on land and on board the *Mya*.

Senator Kennedy, wife Vicki's children, Caroline and Cullan, and Neil walking back up the dock after going out to check the lobster traps.

Scampi with Linguine

SERVES 4 TO 6

EVERYONE LOVES ITALIAN SHRIMP WITH GARLIC. Made the way I do it, with plenty of sauce, it's an excellent topping for linguine, though you could substitute rice.

Since the scampi takes less than 10 minutes to prepare, it's easy to make while the pasta cooks. Begin with a salad and accompany the linguine with a nice green vegetable, such as asparagus or escarole, and Garlic-Cheese Crostini (page 23), if you like.

1 pound linguine
2 tablespoons extra virgin olive oil
1 pound jumbo or extra-large shrimp, peeled and deveined
2 tablespoons all-purpose flour
2 garlic cloves, thinly sliced
½ cup dry sherry
1 teaspoon fresh lemon juice
1 cup fish or chicken stock
2 tablespoons butter, at room temperature
1 tablespoon chopped parsley

1. BRING A LARGE POT of salted water to a boil. Add the linguine and cook until *al dente,* tender but still firm, 10 to 12 minutes. Drain into a colander.

2. WHILE THE PASTA IS COOKING, prepare the scampi: Heat a large sauté pan or skillet over medium-high heat. Add 2 tablespoons olive oil and heat until very hot but not smoking. Quickly dust the shrimp lightly with 1 tablespoon of the flour and add to the pan along with the garlic. Sauté, turning once, until the shrimp are lightly browned on both sides, 2 to 3 minutes.

3. IMMEDIATELY ADD the sherry and lemon juice. With a slotted spoon, remove the shrimp to a bowl. Raise the heat under the skillet to high and add the stock. Boil for 2 minutes to reduce the liquid and intensify the flavors. While this is happening, blend the remaining 1 tablespoon flour into the softened butter to make a smooth paste.

4. WHISK THE BUTTER paste into the boiling sauce. Continue to whisk as it thickens so it's nice and smooth. Reduce the heat to low and simmer for 2 minutes. Return the shrimp and any juices that have collected in the bowl to the pan. Add the cooked linguine and toss to mix. Transfer to a large pasta bowl or serving platter, dust with the parsley, and serve at once.

Pan-Seared Sea Scallops with Shrimp Beurre Blanc

SERVES 4

WHEN I PREPARED THIS SPECIAL-OCCASION DISH for dinner parties at the Compound, I presented the scallops in individual potato baskets. These are charming, but since most people don't like deep-frying when there's company in the house, I suggest serving rice or small orzo pasta as an accompaniment.

Here is my formula for a really colorful vegetable "confetti" garnish: For the rims of four plates: 2 teaspoons each finely diced peeled and seeded tomato, green bell pepper, pitted Kalamata olives, lemon zest, chives, and carrots.

12 to 16 large sea scallops, preferably diver, or dry, scallops
¼ cup all-purpose flour
Salt and freshly ground pepper
2 tablespoons butter
2 tablespoons olive oil
1 garlic clove, minced
1½ teaspoons minced Japanese pickled ginger or 1 teaspoon minced fresh ginger
½ cup dry white wine
1 tablespoon fresh lime juice (save the zest for the sauce recipe that follows)
Shrimp Beurre Blanc (recipe follows)

1. IF ANY OF THE SCALLOPS has a tough "tendon" attached to its side, remove with a small knife.

2. IN A WIDE BOWL, mix the flour with ¼ teaspoon salt and ⅛ teaspoon pepper. Add the scallops and toss to coat lightly.

3. MELT THE BUTTER in the oil in a large ovenproof sauté pan or skillet over medium-high heat. As soon as it is bubbling, add the scallops and sauté until golden brown on the bottom, 2 to 3 minutes. Turn over and sauté for 1 minute. Add the garlic and ginger and continue to cook until the scallops are browned on the second side, 1 to 2 minutes longer. Remove the scallops to a plate.

4. POUR IN THE WINE and lime juice and bring to a boil, scraping up any browned bits from the bottom of the pan. Boil for 1 minute longer to reduce slightly. Return the scallops to the pan and toss to coat with the liquid. Cover and simmer until the scallops are cooked through, 2 to 3 minutes, depending upon size. Be sure not to overcook, or the scallops will toughen.

5. ARRANGE THE SCALLOPS on 4 plates and pour the pan juices on top. Spoon the Shrimp Beurre Blanc over them. Decorate the plate with vegetable confetti, if desired.

Shrimp Beurre Blanc

MAKES ABOUT 1 CUP; ENOUGH FOR 4 SERVINGS

NOTE THAT ALL THE INITIAL STEPS of this recipe can be completed several hours in advance. Once you finish the sauce in Step 3, however, it will not hold and must be used at once.

¼ pound shrimp in their shells
2 shallots, thinly sliced
⅓ cup dry white wine
2 tablespoons white wine vinegar
1 teaspoon minced pickled ginger
¼ teaspoon whole black peppercorns
⅓ cup heavy cream
6 tablespoons butter, at room temperature
2 teaspoons minced fresh chives
½ teaspoon grated lime zest
Salt and freshly ground white pepper

1. SHELL AND DEVEIN THE SHRIMP; reserve the shells. Bring a saucepan of salted water to a boil. Add the shrimp and cook for 1 to 2 minutes, until they are pink and loosely curled. Drain and rinse under cold water to cool them. Finely dice the shrimp and set aside.

2. PUT THE RESERVED SHRIMP SHELLS into a small nonreactive saucepan. Add the shallots, white wine, vinegar, pickled ginger, and whole peppercorns. Boil until the liquid is syrupy and reduced to about 2 tablespoons. Strain into a clean small heavy pot. Add the heavy cream. (The sauce can be prepared to this point up to 3 hours in advance. Cover and refrigerate. When you're ready to serve, proceed to the final step.)

3. BRING THE SHRIMP-FLAVORED CREAM to a boil. Boil for 2 minutes. Immediately remove from the heat and gradually whisk in the butter 1 tablespoon at a time, making sure each piece is just barely incorporated before adding the next. When all the butter is added and the sauce is the consistency of mayonnaise, stir in the diced shrimp, chives, and lime zest. Season with salt and white pepper to taste and serve immediately

"It was always a pleasure when the house filled up with the *scents* of winter: logs burning in the fireplace, cider steeping with cloves, oranges, and anis, and pies and breads in the oven."

Max Kennedy's house in Hyannis Port

Meats *and* Chicken

Filet Mignon with Irish Mist Sauce

SERVES 6

TO SOME PEOPLE, WINTER MAY SEEM OUT OF SEASON at the Cape, but Senator Kennedy sailed all year round, and many of the Kennedys flocked to the Compound in Hyannis for Thanksgiving and Christmas, to spend the holidays with their grandmother Rose. For Christmas, I usually cooked fillet of beef. When I made these sumptuous steaks, I topped each with a slab of sautéed foie gras before spooning on the sauce flavored with Irish spirits. Potatoes au Gratin (page 146) and asparagus with Hollandaise sauce would make fine accompaniments. Dessert was usually a soufflé and sugar cookies.

Filet mignons, small thick tenderloin steaks, which are the leanest and most tender meat you can cook, are elegant and easy for a large group. All the steaks can be browned and the sauce prepared hours ahead. When you begin to serve your first course, simply put the steaks into the oven to finish cooking. It's as simple as that.

6 center-cut filet mignon steaks, cut 2 inches thick
Salt and freshly ground pepper
6 slices of pancetta or bacon
3 tablespoons olive oil
1 medium shallot, minced
¼ cup dry red wine, preferably Cabernet Sauvignon
¼ cup Irish Mist
⅔ cup demi-glace or beef broth
2 tablespoons butter
2 teaspoons all-purpose flour
1 tablespoon chopped parsley

1. SEASON THE FILET MIGNON STEAKS with salt and pepper. Wrap a slice of pancetta around the edge of each steak. Secure with a toothpick to hold it in place.

2. SET A SAUTÉ PAN or large heavy skillet over medium-high heat. Add 1½ tablespoons of the olive oil. When the oil is very hot but not smoking, add the steaks and sear, turning once, until nicely browned, 3 to 4 minutes on each side. Remove the steaks to a small baking sheet. If not finishing at once, let cool slightly; wrap well and refrigerate for up to 6 hours. Let return to room temperature before finishing.

3. RETURN THE SKILLET you just used to medium heat and add the remaining oil. Add the shallot and cook for about 2 minutes to soften. Pour in the wine and Irish Mist and bring to a boil, scraping up any browned bits from the bottom of the pan. Pour in the demi-glace or stock. Boil for 3 to 4 minutes to reduce slightly. (If not serving at once, scrape the sauce into a covered container and refrigerate.)

4. WHEN YOU'RE READY TO SERVE, preheat the oven to 375 degrees F. Arrange the filet mignons on a small baking sheet and bake for 12 to 15 minutes, or until the internal temperature of the meat registers 130 degrees F for medium-rare.

5. WHILE THE STEAKS ARE ROASTING, reheat the sauce to boiling. In a small bowl, blend the butter and flour to make a smooth paste. Swirl into the sauce and continue to boil, whisking, until thickened and smooth. Add the parsley and season with salt and pepper to taste.

6. WHEN THE STEAKS ARE DONE, roll them in the sauce to coat, then arrange on plates or on a platter. Don't forget to remove the toothpick from each filet. Spoon any remaining sauce on top.

Rose's dining room, set up for a dinner buffet.

Hardwood Grilled New York Sirloin Steak

SERVES 4 TO 6

CHEFS HAVE LOTS OF LITTLE TRICKS for adding extra flavor to a dish. Here's one that's easy to copy at home. A simple grilled steak, perfectly cooked, is finished off with a small pat of intensely flavored butter that melts right into the meat.

4 center-cut New York sirloins (USDA Prime or Choice), cut at least 1¼ inches thick, about 12 ounces each

2 tablespoons olive oil

Salt and freshly ground pepper

2 to 3 tablespoons Parsley-Shallot Butter (recipe follows)

1. BRUSH BOTH SIDES of the sirloin steaks with olive oil, then season with salt and pepper.

2. LIGHT A HOT FIRE with hardwood charcoal in a barbecue grill, banking the coals to one side. Or preheat a gas grill set to high.

3. PLACE THE STEAKS on the hot side of the grill and cook, turning once, until nicely browned, 3 to 4 minutes per side. This will sear in the juices of the meat. Do not use a grill fork to turn the steaks. Use a metal spatula so the meat is not punctured.

4. NOW MOVE THE STEAKS to the cooler side of the charcoal grill or reduce the heat on the gas grill to medium-low. Finish the cooking, about 3 to 4 minutes for medium-rare, 130 degrees F. Remove from the grill, top each steak with a slice of the parsley-shallot butter, and serve at once.

Parsley-Shallot Butter

MAKES 4 OUNCES: ENOUGH FOR 8 SERVINGS

Refrigerate or freeze whatever's left of this butter after topping the steaks. It can impart extra flavor to almost any beef or lamb dish or to a grilled or steamed vegetable.

1 stick (4 ounces) butter, slightly softened

2 teaspoons minced shallot

2 teaspoons minced parsley

1 teaspoon fresh lemon juice

¼ teaspoon coarsely cracked black pepper

BLEND TOGETHER ALL THE INGREDIENTS. Scrape onto a sheet of waxed paper and roll into a log. Wrap well and refrigerate until chilled and set. (The butter will keep well in the refrigerator for up to 3 days or in the freezer for up to 2 months.)

Marinated London Broil

SERVES 4 TO 6

WHILE MANY CUTS OF MEAT have been called "London broil," the classic cut is the sirloin flank. Choice grade will give you the best flavor. Grilled London broil is wonderful with salad right on the same plate; the flavorful meat juices help dress the greens. At the Compound, of course, there were always sliced beefsteak tomatoes on the plate in summer.

1 flank steak, about 2 pounds
½ cup olive oil
¼ cup tomato sauce
¼ cup balsamic vinegar
2 tablespoons fresh lemon juice
1 teaspoon dried thyme or tarragon leaves
Salt and freshly ground pepper
¼ cup finely chopped onion
1 garlic clove, minced

1. TRIM ANY EXCESS FAT from the steak. Lay flat in a large glass baking dish.

2. IN A MEDIUM BOWL, whisk together the olive oil, tomato sauce, balsamic vinegar, lemon juice, thyme, ½ teaspoon salt, and ¼ teaspoon pepper. Stir in the onion and garlic. Pour over the meat, cover, and let stand at room temperature, turning once, for 1 hour, or refrigerate for up to 3 hours

3. LIGHT A HOT FIRE with hardwood charcoal in a barbecue grill, banking the coals to one side. Or preheat a gas grill set to high.

4. REMOVE THE FLANK STEAK from its marinade and briefly pat dry on paper towels. Grill for 3 to 4 minutes, rotating the steak 45 degrees after about 2 minutes to create cross-hatch grill marks. Turn the steak over and repeat on the second side.

5. SLIDE THE MEAT to the cooler side of the grill or lower the heat on a gas grill to medium-low, and finish cooking for 3 to 4 minutes longer, until the steak is rare or medium-rare. Flank steak gets tough if it is well done.

6. REMOVE THE MEAT to a cutting board and let it rest, loosely covered with foil, for about 5 minutes. Using a long sharp knife, carve into thin slices against the grain on a slight angle, so the pieces of meat are about 1½ inches wide.

Chef's Note: A good tip when cooking any steak or chop is to always use a pair of tongs or a metal spatula instead of a fork to turn the meat so no juices are lost during the cooking process. Also, make sure you pull the meat out of the refrigerator about 20 minutes before cooking so it is not ice cold when you place it on the hot grill.

Meat Loaf

SERVES 6 TO 8

EVERYONE LOVES MEAT LOAF, and the Kennedys were no exception. It's comfort food that I often served in winter, accompanied by mashed potatoes and green beans. I don't usually brag, but many people have told me that my meat loaf, which as you can see is complexly flavored, is the best they've ever tasted. And by the way, don't worry about that long list of ingredients. They all go in one bowl and into the oven in less than 10 minutes.

This meat loaf is good hot, room temperature, or cold. In fact, one of the Senator's favorite sandwiches was cold meat loaf on a Portuguese roll or Italian bread with ketchup. Come to think if it, that's one of my favorite sandwiches, too.

2 pounds ground sirloin
¾ cup finely chopped onion
½ cup finely chopped green bell pepper
2 garlic cloves, finely chopped
1½ cups dry bread crumbs
3 eggs
1 cup grated Parmesan cheese
¾ cup marinara sauce (use your favorite brand)
⅓ cup milk
1 tablespoon chopped fresh basil or parsley
1 tablespoon chopped fresh oregano or 1 teaspoon dried
2 tablespoons Worcestershire sauce
2 tablespoons A-1 Steak Sauce
2 splashes of Tabasco
Glaze: ½ cup ketchup, 1 tablespoon brown sugar, and 1 teaspoon cider vinegar

1. PREHEAT THE OVEN to 350 degrees F.

2. IN A LARGE BOWL combine the ground meat with the onion, bell pepper, garlic, bread crumbs, eggs, Parmesan cheese, marinara sauce, milk, basil, oregano, Worcestershire sauce, steak sauce, and Tabasco. Mix, preferably with your hands, until very well blended.

3. EITHER PACK THE MEAT mixture into two 9 by 5 by 3-inch loaf pans or mold it into one freeform loaf on a large baking sheet. It is important to press and smooth the meatloaf so it keeps its shape.

4. MAKE A GLAZE by mixing together the ketchup, brown sugar, and vinegar. Using a pastry brush, brush the top of each meat loaf evenly.

5. BAKE THE MEAT loaves or the single large loaf for 55 to 60 minutes, or until nicely browned outside and cooked through.

Mushroom, Gorgonzola, and Bacon Burgers

SERVES 4

YES, EVEN THE KENNEDYS ATE HAMBURGERS upon occasion. As you can see from this recipe, they preferred them pan-fried rather than grilled, so that the meat would develop a nice even brown crust, sealing in the juices and enhancing the taste. The children liked them plain or as simple cheeseburgers, but my super-enhanced burgers with sautéed mushrooms and gorgonzola cheese were in demand by everyone over the age of 12.

1½ pounds ground sirloin
Salt and freshly ground pepper
8 thick slices of smoked bacon
6 ounces mushrooms, sliced (about 1 cup)
1 tablespoon butter
4 ounces gorgonzola cheese, crumbled
4 leaves of green leaf lettuce
4 slices of beefsteak tomato
4 kaiser or other crusty rolls, toasted
4 slices of red onion

1. PREHEAT THE OVEN to 375 degrees F. Season the ground meat with salt and pepper and handling it lightly, form into 4 patties about ½ inch thick.

2. PLACE THE BACON on a baking sheet. Cook in the oven for for 8 to 10 minutes, or until lightly browned. Drain on paper towels.

3. SET A LARGE HEAVY SKILLET, preferably cast iron, over medium heat. When the pan is hot, add the burgers. Cook until nicely browned on the bottom, about 4 to 5 minutes. Turn over and cook until browned on the second side. Reduce the heat to medium and continue to cook until the meat reaches the desired degree of doneness, 3 to 5 minutes. Here's a chef's tip: Use an instant-read or digital thermometer to measure the internal temperature: 130 degrees F will be rare to medium-rare.

4. WHILE THE BURGERS ARE COOKING, in a medium skillet, sauté the mushrooms in the butter over medium-high heat until golden brown, about 5 minutes; drain off any excess moisture. Crumble the gorgonzola into the skillet and mix with the mushrooms; remove from the heat.

5. TO ASSEMBLE EACH BURGER, place a lettuce leaf and slice of tomato on the bottom half of a roll. Add a burger. Cover with with one fourth of the mushrooms and gorgonzola, 2 slices of crisp bacon, a slice of red onion, and finally the top of the toasted roll.

HOLIDAY GATHERINGS ON THE CAPE

When and where are you the happiest?" *Vanity Fair* magazine asked Senator Kennedy this question not long ago. I would have guessed he'd answer, "On board the *Mya* in July." I was wrong. His answer was simple and touching: "Every Thanksgiving when our family gathers on Cape Cod," he said.

There is no question that his family's Hyannis Port house was made for the long, sun-filled days of summer, warm sea breezes, a game of tennis, an afternoon sail to Nantucket. But the houses on the Compound are open all year long, anise, and pies and breads in the oven. And with visitors we hadn't seen since summer. They would come through the kitchen door wearing scarves and ski jackets, bearing gifts and good cheer. The days were short and the weather not always inviting, but the familiar comforts and traditions kept everyone in high spirits. So, too, did the Kennedys' generosity to others in Hyannis and on Cape Cod. Throughout the holiday season, they donated thousands of meals and gifts to senior citizens and children through churches, community centers, and schools. Every year, I worked with a group of local chefs

"The days were short and the weather not always inviting, but the

and the Kennedys are extraordinarily close knit across many generations. The Senator has always been as much a father as an uncle to his two late brothers' children—Caroline and John Jr. and Bobby and Ethel's eleven sons and daughters. In my years as his chef, it was the Senator who orchestrated Thanksgiving and Christmas at the Compound, who made sure far-flung children, nieces, and nephews came back from wherever they were to gather in his childhood dining room for holiday meals.

It was always a pleasure when the house filled up with the scents of winter: logs burning in the fireplace, cider steeping with cloves, oranges, and

cooking holiday meals in the public schools.

Even at that time of year, the Senator loved to sail. It wasn't at all unusual for him to take the *Mya* over to Nantucket for an afternoon—supplied with plenty of my hot clam chowder. Over Thanksgiving dinner, guests often discussed who would be going on the Nantucket Stroll two weeks later, a favorite family activity. On the first weekend of every December, the island hosts a celebration where downtown is turned over to carolers, brass bands, and Santa Claus arriving on a Coast Guard cutter and riding into town in a horse drawn carriage. Main Street is closed to cars, the shops are open, and visitors often stay for the play on Saturday night—*A Child's Christmas in Wales* and *A Christmas Carol* are favorites—and a choral concert in one of the churches on Sunday morning.

Weeks later, on Christmas day, as family members streamed through the kitchen door, careful to close it against the cold, their excitement was palpable. Soon I'd hear the oohs and aahs of presents being opened in the living room, singing, piano playing, and stories being told over trills of laughter.

As I put the finishing touches on the dining room table, I would look into the living room. Wrapping paper and ribbons were everywhere. The sight of the tree in the corner always brought to mind the story I'd heard about Rose Kennedy's father's special contribution to the holiday. When he was mayor of Boston, he started what came to be a tradition of putting a large decorated Christmas tree in the Boston Common, for families too poor to have their own. This gesture spread throughout the country and became the beginning of Christmas trees in public spaces, which Rockefeller Center would carry on with its famous tree that goes up every year in New York.

familiar comforts and traditions kept everyone in high spirits."

I caught myself smiling at this lovely piece of family history and American history and hurried back to the kitchen. It was almost time for dinner. Later that day, when the Kennedys were finished with their Christmas meal, I'd go home and celebrate this special day with my own family.

FACING PAGE: *The Senator with nephew John Jr. and son Patrick in* Le Grand Fromage, *the motor launch used to run out to the* Mya, *which was anchored in deep water.*
ABOVE: *Senator Kennedy walking down the dock after a winter sail with nephew Max Kennedy, one of Robert Kennedy's sons.*
LEFT: *Just before Christmas: the decorated tree in Rose's living room, waiting for presents.*

Spinach-Stuffed Veal Chops with Port Wine Sauce

SERVES 4

ADMITTEDLY, VEAL CHOPS ARE LUXURIOUS, but they're a real treat for entertaining. The best part of this recipe is that the chops can be stuffed and even browned in advance, and the dish finished at the last minute with little fuss. When I cooked this for the Kennedys, I usually served it with a Saffron Risotto (page 157). You could easily substitute plain or wild rice.

4 veal rib chops, cut ¾ inch thick, about 8 ounces each
Spinach Stuffing (recipe follows)
½ cup plus 1 tablespoon all-purpose flour
Salt and freshly ground pepper
¼ cup olive oil
2 tablespoons butter, at room temperature
1 medium shallot, chopped
⅔ cup port wine
1 cup beef stock
½ teaspoon grated lemon zest
1 tablespoon fresh lemon juice, or more to taste

1. PREHEAT THE OVEN to 375 degrees F. Make a 1½-inch cut in the meaty edge of the veal chops and wiggle the knife to enlarge the pocket without cutting through the meat. Spoon the stuffing into the pockets of the veal chops. Secure the edges with wooden toothpicks. Mix ½ cup of the flour with ½ teaspoon salt and ¼ teaspoon pepper and use to dust both sides of each chop.

2. IN A LARGE SKILLET heat the olive oil over medium-high heat. Place the chops in the hot oil and brown, turning once, 4 to 5 minutes per side. Transfer the veal chops to a baking sheet; set the skillet aside without rinsing it.

3. ROAST THE CHOPS in the oven for 12 to 15 minutes, or until tender and no longer pink in the center but still juicy.

4. WHILE THE CHOPS BAKE, make the port wine sauce: Melt 1 tablespoon of the butter in the skillet used to brown the chops. Add the shallot and cook over medium heat until beginning to color, 3 to 4 minutes. Add the port and boil for 1 minute, scraping up any brown bits from the bottom of the pan. Add the stock, lemon zest, and lemon juice.

5. MIX THE REMAINING 1 tablespoon flour with the remaining 1 tablespoon butter to make a smooth paste. Stir into the sauce. Return to a boil and cook for 2 minutes, whisking until smooth and slightly thickened. Season with additional salt and pepper and perhaps more lemon juice to taste. Spoon some of the sauce onto each plate. Put a stuffed veal chop on top and drizzle the remaining sauce over the meat.

Spinach Stuffing

MAKES ABOUT 2 CUPS

3 tablespoons butter or olive oil
4 ounces fresh shiitake mushrooms, stemmed, caps sliced
5 ounces washed baby spinach (½ bag)
½ cup chopped prosciutto
1 tablespoon sliced shallot
1 teaspoon minced garlic
1 cup grated Parmesan cheese
3 ounces Boursin cheese
½ cup bread crumbs

1. IN A SAUTÉ PAN or in a large skillet, melt the butter over medium-high heat. Add the shiitake mushrooms and the spinach and sauté, stirring for about 2 minutes.

2. ADD THE CHOPPED PROSCIUTTO, shallot, and garlic. Cook, tossing to wilt the spinach, for 1 to 2 minutes longer. Remove from the stove and place in a medium bowl.

3. STIR IN THE PARMESAN CHEESE, Boursin cheese, and bread crumbs. Cover and refrigerate until ready to use.

Variation

Spinach-Stuffed Pork Chops: In place of the veal, use 4 double-thick boneless pork chops. After browning, roast the stuffed chops for 15 minutes, or until the meat registers 145 to 155 degrees F.

Chef's Note: While the rule of thumb when choosing a wine to cook with is to pick a red or white that you wouldn't mind drinking with the dish, fortified wines like port and Madeira offer more leeway. Personally, if I'm going to drink a glass of port, say after dinner with some freshly cracked walnuts and a wedge of Stilton cheese, I'd like it to be a serious vintage port or a late-harvest that has been aged for at least 10 years. For cooking, though, since I just want a hint of that plummy flavor, I'll use a relatively inexpensive ruby port or tawny port—whichever I happen to have on hand.

Veal Scallopine Nantucket-Style

SERVES 4

SINCE IT WAS SO FRESH AND GOOD TASTING and all the Kennedys loved it, seafood was served every which way at the Compound. In this recipe, sea scallops are perched atop breaded veal scallops. The seafood is topped off with a dollop of orange-flavored Hollandaise sauce. I usually served the dish with steamed or sautéed asparagus and rice or noodles.

1 pound veal scallops, pounded thin
3 eggs
½ cup dry Marsala
¾ cup all-purpose flour
Salt and freshly ground pepper
¾ cup bread crumbs
¼ cup plus 2 tablespoons olive oil
1 garlic clove, minced
⅔ cup chicken broth
8 large sea scallops, cut horizontally in half
Orange Hollandaise Sauce (page 116)

1. IN A WIDE SHALLOW BOWL, beat the eggs with 2 tablespoons of the Marsala to make an egg wash. In another bowl, mix the flour with ½ teaspoon salt and ⅛ teaspoon pepper. Put the bread crumbs in a third shallow bowl.

2. LIGHTLY DUST THE VEAL SCALLOPS with the seasoned flour; shake off and reserve the excess. Dip the veal in the egg wash and then dredge in the bread crumbs to coat both sides evenly.

3. IN A SAUTÉ PAN or large skillet, heat ¼ cup of the olive oil until hot. Add the veal, in batches if necessary, and sauté over medium-high heat, turning once, until golden brown on both sides, 4 to 5 minutes total. Remove the veal scallops to a platter; cover to warm.

4. ADD THE GARLIC to the pan and cook for 1 to 2 minutes to soften slightly. Pour in the remaining 6 tablespoons Marsala. Bring to a boil, scraping up any brown bits from the bottom of the pan. Boil until reduced by half. Add the stock and boil for 2 to 3 minutes to reduce slightly.

5. IN A SEPARATE SKILLET, preferably cast iron, heat the remaining 2 tablespoons oil until hot over medium-high heat. Dust the scallops with the reserved seasoned flour to coat both sides lightly, then add them to the hot pan. Brown quickly, 2 to 3 minutes on each side.

6. TO ASSEMBLE, ladle a few tablespoons of the sauce onto each plate. Top with a veal scallop. Arrange the scallops on top of the veal and dollop a heaping tablespoon of Orange Hollandaise on top.

Orange Hollandaise Sauce

MAKES ABOUT 1½ CUPS

IN CLASSIC FRENCH COOKING, this preparation is known as Sauce Maltaise. It is traditionally paired with asparagus, which is one reason I suggest serving asparagus as your green vegetable with the veal on the previous page. The orange also goes beautifully with the scallops. My secret here is blood orange juice. While you see these burgundy-fleshed fruits in markets all over now, they are highly seasonal, and regular juice oranges can be used as well.

3 egg yolks

2 sticks (8 ounces) butter, melted and cooled slightly

1½ tablespoons fresh orange juice, preferably blood orange

½ teaspoon grated orange zest

Salt and ground white pepper

1. WHISK THE EGG YOLKS in a double boiler or a stainless steel bowl set over simmering water. Continue to whisk until the eggs just begin to thicken, 2 to 3 minutes; do not let them scramble.

2. IMMEDIATELY REMOVE from the heat and very gradually begin to add the melted butter a few drops a time, whisking constantly. After the first couple of tablespoons, the sauce should begin to emulsify and thicken. At that point, beat in the orange juice. Then continue whisking in the butter in a slow, thin stream, stopping before you add the solid fat at the bottom.

3. BEAT IN THE ORANGE zest and season the sauce with salt and white pepper to taste. Use at once or set aside for up to 30 minutes, until ready for use. Keep warm near the stove, but do not heat or the butter will separate.

Chef's Note: The secret to a successful Hollandaise sauce is to be sure all your ingredients are at room temperature before you make the emulsion. If you're afraid to leave eggs out, simply dip in a bowl of hot water for a minute or two to warm them up before beginning. Melt your butter 5 or 10 minutes in advance and let it cool to tepid.

Also, make sure you whisk in the butter very slowly. If your sauce starts to separate, don't panic. Pour the "broken" Hollandaise into a blender, add a teaspoon of water, and blend at high speed until it becomes thick and smooth. The sauce should be served just slightly warm, not hot.

Grilled Pork Chops

SERVES 4

PORK CHOPS ARE AMAZINGLY VERSATILE. Sometimes I'd grill them after marinating in the Asian-flavored sauce below, which make them extremely succulent. Other times, I'd use the marinade for the London broil on page 106. Either way, I often served them with Andouille Mashed Potatoes (page 145) and grilled zucchini.

4 bone-in pork loin chops, cut 1 inch thick, 7 to 8 ounces each

⅓ cup vegetable oil

3 tablespoons rice vinegar

2 tablespoons Asian sesame oil

2 tablespoons soy sauce

2 garlic cloves, minced

1 tablespoon chopped pickled ginger

1 tablespoon chopped parsley

1. TRIM any excess fat from the chops. In a glass or ceramic baking dish, combine the vegetable oil, vinegar, sesame oil, soy sauce, garlic, ginger, and parsley. Add the pork chops and turn to coat. Marinate them, turning occasionally, for at least 2 hours in the refrigerator.

2. LIGHT A HOT FIRE with hardwood charcoal in a barbecue grill, banking the coals to one side. Or preheat a gas grill set to high.

3. REMOVE THE CHOPS from the marinade and pat dry with paper towels. You don't want the oil from the marinade to flare up over the coals. Grill the chops for about 4 minutes, until nicely browned on the bottom. Turn over with a metal spatula—not a fork!—and brown the second side, about 4 minutes.

4. NOW MOVE the chops to the cooler side of the grill, or reduce the heat on a gas grill to medium-low to finish the cooking. Close the lid on the grill and check periodically. This final cooking should take about 5 to 6 minutes, until the meat is white throughout but still moist.

Barbecued Baby-Back Ribs

SERVES 4 TO 6

THESE WERE A HUGE HIT at many of the big barbecues the Kennedys threw all summer long. The kids particularly loved them. But, then, so did the grown-ups. Serve with potato salad, corn-on-the cob, sliced garden tomatoes, and a big green salad.

3 racks of baby-back ribs, trimmed of excess fat
½ cup Worcestershire sauce
1 teaspoon dried basil
1 teaspoon ground ginger
1 teaspoon granulated garlic
1 teaspoon granulated onion
1 teaspoon salt
½ teaspoon black pepper
½ teaspoon ground cinnamon
¼ teaspoon ground cloves
1½ cups barbecue sauce, preferably my No-Cook Barbecue Sauce (recipe follows)

1. BRUSH THE RIBS generously all over with Worcestershire sauce. Set them in a large baking dish. Mix together the basil, ginger, granulated garlic and onion, salt, pepper, cinnamon, and cloves. Rub the seasoning mix all over the ribs. Cover and marinate in the refrigerator for at least 1 hour or preferably overnight.

2. PREHEAT THE OVEN to 375 degrees F. Bake the ribs uncovered for 1 hour, turning once. (The ribs can be prepared to this point up to a day in advance.) Let them return to room temperature before proceeding.

3. LIGHT A HOT FIRE in a charcoal grill, banking the coals to one side. Or preheat a gas grill set to high. Grill the ribs over the hot coals for about 4 minutes a side to brown nicely. Then slide them to the cooler side of the grill or reduce the heat on a gas grill to medium-low.

4. SLATHER THE RIBS with barbecue sauce, basting both sides. Continue to grill for 10 to 12 minutes, turning and basting, until extremely tender and nicely glazed.

Chef's Note: Because the ribs are completely cooked in advance, you don't have to worry about them at all once they reach the grill. My easy barbecue sauce, which I highly recommend, can be made weeks in advance.

No-Cook Barbecue Sauce

MAKES ABOUT 1 QUART

THIS ALL-PURPOSE GINGERY SAUCE is excellent on many foods: pork, shrimp, chicken, and beef. Whenever I make it, I always put up a big batch, because the sauce not only keeps well for up to a month in the refrigerator, it continues to improve as the flavors mellow.

3 cups ketchup
1 cup orange juice, preferably fresh
¾ cup cider vinegar
½ cup packed brown sugar
3 tablespoons honey
3 tablespoons Worcestershire sauce
¼ cup A-1 Steak Sauce
2 tablespoons minced fresh ginger
3 garlic cloves, crushed through a press
½ teaspoon Tabasco sauce

WHISK all the ingredients together in a bowl. Refrigerate for at least 2 hours and preferably overnight before using.

Mustard-Crusted Rack of Lamb

SERVES 4 TO 6

BACK WHEN I COOKED FOR THE KENNEDYS, rack of lamb was an extravagance you could only get at restaurants and from special order at a good butcher shop. Now rack of lamb is found in many supermarkets—much of it imported from Australia and New Zealand, where the animals are raised on grass, with no antibiotics or hormones. Next to fillet of beef, it's the easiest and quickest luxury roast you can cook. Serve with Potatoes au Gratin (page 146) and Green Beans with Morels (page 140).

2 racks of lamb, 12 to 16 ounces each
1 tablespoon extra virgin olive oil
Coarse salt and freshly ground pepper
3 tablespoons coarse French "Pommery" mustard
½ cup fresh bread crumbs

1. IF THE RACKS are prepackaged, chances are they are already "frenched." This means all the fat has been removed from the long rib bones, which makes for a much more attractive roast. If you're buying it from a butcher, ask him to french the racks and to make sure the bones are cleaned well.

2. HEAT THE OLIVE OIL in a hot sauté pan or large skillet. Place the racks of lamb meaty side down in the hot pan and sear over medium-high heat until nicely browned on that one side, about 5 minutes. If your pan is too small and you have to do this in 2 batches, wipe out the pan and use fresh oil for the second rack. Remove the racks to a platter and let cool for about 10 minutes.

3. WHEN THE RACKS are cool enough to handle, rub the meat all over with the salt and pepper. Using a pastry brush, spread the mustard over the browned meat part only, leaving the bones clean.

4. NOW COVER THE MEAT with the fresh bread crumbs, patting them lightly to help them adhere. The mustard will make them stick to the meat. (The recipe can be prepared to this point up to 6 hours in advance. Wrap the racks of lamb and refrigerate. Return to room temperature about 1 hour before roasting.)

5. PREHEAT THE OVEN to 375 degrees F. Place the racks, meaty side up, on a baking sheet and roast for 15 to 20 minutes, depending on the doneness you desire. Remove from the oven and let the meat rest for 4 to 5 minutes. Using a sharp knife, slice between the bones to separate each rack into 2 or 3 servings of several chops each.

THE KENNEDYS' IRISH PRIDE

Rose Fitzgerald Kennedy was the daughter of a man known as "Honey Fitz," the first mayor of Boston to have had immigrant parents. His mother and father fled Ireland after the devastating potato famines, in the 1860s, and they arrived in a city where the established society—Boston's Brahmin blue bloods—wanted nothing to do with them. A hundred years later, Honey Fitz's grandson, John Fitzgerald Kennedy, became the most powerful man in the world, and the country's first Irish Catholic president.

When the President visited Ireland in the summer of 1963, he said it was "one of the most moving experiences" of his life. He felt such a connection to the country and its people that he expressed the hope that he would one day be the U.S. ambassador to Ireland—a touching ambition for the man who was President!

He made the trip with his sister Jean Smith. The two Kennedys toured the land, as enraptured with its countrymen and women as the Irish were with them. We think of Kennedy's election in 1960 as a milestone for Irish Catholics in the United States, but it was also a turning point for the Irish themselves—one of their own was now a world leader.

"I prepared a brunch for the Prime Minister of Ireland, Charles Haughey,

ABOVE: *Senator Kennedy and the Irish Prime Minister (left) at a brunch in the dining room of "The President's House." Note Jackie's collection of cobalt Sandwich glass at upper left.*
FACING PAGE: *Neil chatting with Irish Prime Minister Charles Haughey in the kitchen of Rose Kennedy's house during a weekend visit.*

Although Jackie Kennedy could not accompany her husband because she was pregnant, she later spoke movingly about the trip and his connection to the country. "It wasn't just a sentimental journey," she said. "Ireland meant much more." Despite his privileged upbringing, the President identified deeply with the tragic struggle of his ancestors—their poverty, political oppression, and separation from their homeland—and with their celebrated penchant for creating poetry and song out of the depths of despair.

which was served in the dining room of The President's House."

The Kennedys' official connections to Ireland deepened as time went by. In 1964, Joan Kennedy, then the Senator's wife, toured the country and was received with nearly the same enthusiasm that had greeted the President and his sister the year before. Decades later, Jean Smith would fulfill her brother's dream and be appointed Ambassador to Ireland by President Clinton. During her time there, she would be influential in changing United States foreign policy and helping pave the way for peace in Northern Ireland.

If those were the formal ties that bound the Kennedys to their ancestral home, in their everyday lives, they expressed their affection for Ireland in myriad ways. The Senator and his family frequently vacationed there. When Jackie Kennedy took her two children there in 1967, a crowd greeted them at Shannon Airport and warmed to her graciousness. Her husband had loved Ireland so much, she said, that she felt as though she and her children were "coming home."

At family gatherings on Cape Cod, the family often gathered around the baby grand in Rose's living room and sang Irish folk songs: "My Wild Irish Rose" was a specialty of Senator Ted Kennedy's. And on St. Patrick's Day, I was often asked to cook recipes from the "old sod," like lamb stew, Irish bread pudding, and champ or boxity (both potato dishes). Especially in winter, Irish coffee might be served after dinner.

Whenever possible, when Irish dignitaries came to the United States, the family hosted them at the Compound in Hyannis Port. I once prepared a rollicking brunch for the Prime Minister of Ireland, Charles Haughey, which was served in the dining room of The President's House. That was part of a weekend affair, which also included boat lunches, dinners, and, of course, the famous Kennedy clambake.

Irish Lamb Stew

SERVES 6

THE KENNEDYS LOVED MUSHROOMS, so you'll find them in lots of dishes here, including this savory stew. Chock full of tender lamb and an assortment of vegetables, it's a one-dish meal, which needs nothing more than a nice green salad and perhaps some French bread to accompany it. Like almost all stews, this dish improves upon reheating.

1 small shoulder of lamb (4½ pounds), boned with bones reserved for the stock that follows

Salt and freshly ground pepper

4 tablespoons butter

2 medium onions, coarsely chopped

2 garlic cloves, chopped

3 carrots, peeled and thickly sliced

8 ounces white button mushrooms, trimmed and halved

⅓ cup all-purpose flour

Easy Lamb Stock (recipe follows)

3 sprigs of fresh thyme or 1 teaspoon dried leaves

1 bay leaf

3 medium boiling potatoes, peeled and cut into ½-inch dice

1 medium turnip, peeled and cut into ½-inch dice

1. CUT THE LAMB into 1-inch cubes. Pat dry. Season the meat with salt and pepper.

2. MELT THE BUTTER in a large flameproof casserole over medium heat. Add the lamb, onions, garlic, carrots, and mushrooms. Cook, stirring occasionally, until the onion begins to soften, 4 to 5 minutes.

3. SPRINKLE THE FLOUR into the pan and cook, stirring, for 1 to 2 minutes. Slowly add enough stock to cover (about 5 cups), the thyme, and the bay leaf. Stir well and simmer over low heat for about 1 hour. If the liquid evaporates too quickly, add the remaining stock.

4. MEANWHILE, COOK the potatoes and turnip together in a large saucepan of boiling salted water until tender but firm, about 10 minutes. Drain into a colander and rinse briefly under cold running water. Add the potatoes and turnips to the stew and simmer for about 5 minutes to blend the flavors.

Easy Lamb Stock

MAKES ABOUT 6 CUPS

Bones from a 4½ pound lamb shoulder along with any trimmings

2 celery ribs, cut into 1-inch pieces

1 onion, quartered

1 carrot, peeled and quartered

¼ cup tomato paste

1. PREHEAT THE OVEN to 375 degrees F.

2. ARRANGE THE LAMB bones and any trimmings in a roasting pan. Add the celery, onion, and carrot. Roast for 25 to 35 minutes, or until the bones are nicely browned.

3. POUR OFF ANY EXCESS fat and transfer the bones and vegetables to a stockpot or large saucepan. Pour 2 cups water into the roasting pan and bring to a boil on top of the stove, scraping up any browned bits from the bottom of the pan. Pour the liquid into the pot. Add 2½ quarts more water.

4. BRING TO A BOIL and stir in the tomato paste. Reduce the heat and let the stock simmer for 1 hour. Strain and return to the pot. Boil, skimming off any fat from the top, until the liquid is reduced to 6 cups.

North End Chicken in a Pot

SERVES 4

THE NORTH END OF BOSTON IS THE NEIGHBORHOOD where Rose lived as a young woman. Her church remains there. At the turn of the century, it was an Irish and Italian neighborhood. Today, it's largely Italian and famous for its Italian food.

Here's my contemporary version of chicken cacciatore, which is ideal for a family meal. Serve over linguine and pass grated Parmesan cheese on the side. The Garlic-Cheese Crostini on page 23 would be outstanding with this. All you need is a crisp green salad and a bottle of Chianti to make everyone happy.

1 chicken, 2½ to 3 pounds, cut into 8 serving pieces
Salt and freshly ground pepper
2 tablespoons extra virgin olive oil
1 medium onion, coarsely chopped
1 medium green bell pepper, cut into ¾-inch dice
8 ounces fresh shiitake or cremini mushrooms, stemmed and sliced
3 garlic cloves, chopped
½ cup dry white wine
2 cans (14½ ounces each) diced plum tomatoes, with their juices
1 tablespoon chopped fresh basil

1. TRIM ANY EXCESS FAT from the chicken. Rinse and pat dry. Season with salt and pepper.

2. IN A LARGE, HEAVY NONREACTIVE POT, heat the olive oil over medium-high heat. Add the chicken and sauté, turning, until evenly browned all over, about 8 to 10 minutes. Remove to a plate and set aside.

3. ADD THE ONION, bell pepper, mushrooms, and garlic to the pot. Cook, stirring often, until they become soft, about 5 minutes. Add the white wine, the diced tomatoes with their juices, and the basil. Stir to mix well.

4. RETURN THE CHICKEN to the pot, cover, and reduce the heat to medium-low. Simmer for 50 to 60 minutes, stirring occasionally, until the chicken is so tender, it is almost falling off the bone.

Roast Chicken with Fresh Basil and Garlic

SERVES 3 TO 4

NO MATTER WHAT WAS GOING ON in the house, I always kept at least one roast chicken on hand in the refrigerator for snacks, sandwiches, and boat lunches. If I turned around, they always seemed to disappear, even in the middle of the night.

1 whole chicken, about 3 pounds
2 garlic cloves, finely chopped
3 tablespoons chopped fresh basil
¼ cup extra virgin olive oil
1 teaspoon coarse salt
1 teaspoon freshly ground black pepper

1. RINSE THE CHICKEN well inside and out under cold running water. Let drain, then pat dry with paper towels.

2. IN SMALL BOWL, mix together the garlic, basil, and olive oil. Rub over the outside of the chicken and in the cavity. Season inside and out with the salt and pepper. If you have time, refrigerate for 2 or 3 hours so the flavors penetrate.

3. PREHEAT THE OVEN to 350 degrees F. Roast the chicken for 1 hour and 10 to 15 minutes, or until cooked through but still juicy. When the thickest part of the thigh is pricked with a small knife, the juices should run clear.

Chef's Note: Organic chickens are raised without chemicals, hormones, or antibiotics. Free range means the birds are allowed some room to move around, so they can actually build some natural muscles. Because of all these factors, the meat is firmer, much more flavorful, and usually much fresher tasting than ordinary chicken. I recommend buying organic free-range products whenever you can.

Coconut-Crusted Chicken with Mango Cream

SERVES 4

ONE YEAR, AFTER THE HOLIDAYS, we flew down to St. Croix. The Senator had an attachment to the island, because his brother President John F. Kennedy had worked to protect the coral reefs off the coast. For sentimental reasons, he wanted to propose to his now-wife Vicki there. In a most romantic gesture, he took her snorkeling, having planted a gorgeous diamond and sapphire engagement ring right on the ocean floor, and led her to discover it. Needless to say, she was delighted.

All the Senator's children were down there with them—Teddy Jr. and his wife Kiki, Kara and her husband, Michael, and Patrick. I served this chicken to the family that festive evening, accompanied by the Mango-Pineapple Slaw that follows.

4 skinless, boneless chicken breast halves (5 to 6 ounces each), lightly pounded
2 eggs
2 tablespoons dry white wine
⅓ cup tablespoon all-purpose flour
Salt and freshly ground pepper
1½ cups shredded unsweetened coconut
¼ cup vegetable oil
1 mango
¼ cup heavy cream
1 tablespoon honey
Mango-Pineapple Slaw (recipe follows)

1. PREHEAT THE OVEN to 350 degrees F. In a wide shallow bowl, beat the eggs with the wine. Put the flour in another shallow bowl and season with ¼ teaspoon salt and ⅛ teaspoon pepper. Put the coconut in another bowl or in a pie plate.

2. DREDGE THE CHICKEN BREASTS in the seasoned flour; shake off any excess. Then dip in the egg wash to coat, letting excess drip back into the bowl. Dredge in the coconut to coat well all over.

3. HEAT THE OIL in a sauté pan or large skillet over medium-high heat. Add the coated chicken breasts and sauté for 3 to 4 minutes per side, until the crust is golden brown. Transfer to a baking sheet and finish in the oven for 10 to 12 minutes.

4. MEANWHILE, MAKE THE MANGO CREAM sauce: Peel the mango, cut the fruit off the pit, and puree it in a blender or food processor. Pour the cream into a medium saucepan and boil over high heat until reduced to ⅓ cup, 2 to 3 minutes. Stir in the mango puree and the honey. Reduce the heat to low and simmer for 2 minutes longer.

Mango-Pineapple Slaw

MAKES ABOUT 3 CUPS

½ cup mayonnaise
2 tablespoons sugar
2 tablespoons cider vinegar
½ cup coarsely chopped fresh pineapple (reserve any juices on the cutting board)
2 cups finely shredded green cabbage
1 mango, peeled, pitted, and cut into thin strips
1 tablespoon chopped cilantro or parsley

1. IN LARGE BOWL, whisk together the mayonnaise, sugar, vinegar, and any pineapple juices. Then stir in the chopped pineapple.

2. ADD THE CABBAGE, mango, and cilantro. Toss to coat evenly. Cover and refrigerate until chilled.

I served my Coconut-Crusted Chicken with Mango Cream (page 131) with the Mango-Pineapple Slaw (above) to the family the day the Senator proposed to wife Vicki, shown above with John Jr.

Breast of Chicken with Mushrooms and Spinach

SERVES 4 TO 6

HAVING THE EGG ON THE OUTSIDE makes for a very light coating. Serve this savory dish with mashed potatoes.

6 chicken breast halves, 5 to 6 ounces each
2 eggs
¼ plus ⅓ cup Chardonnay or other dry white wine
⅓ cup all-purpose flour
Salt and freshly ground pepper
2 tablespoons olive oil
3 tablespoons butter
1 medium shallot, minced
10 ounces white button mushrooms, sliced
1 package (12 ounces) prewashed baby spinach
½ cup chicken stock
Juice of 1 lemon
1 tablespoon chopped fresh tarragon or 1½ teaspoons dried

1. GENTLY POUND THE CHICKEN breasts between two sheets of waxed paper to flatten evenly.

2. IN A WIDE SHALLOW BOWL, whisk the eggs with ¼ cup Chardonnay to make an egg wash. In another bowl, mix together the flour with ¼ teapoon salt and a pinch of pepper.

3. DREDGE THE CHICKEN breasts in the seasoned flour to coat both sides. Shake any excess back into the bowl. Then dip in the egg wash to coat all over and let soak until ready to cook.

4. HEAT A SAUTÉ PAN or large skillet over medium-high heat. When hot, add the olive oil. As soon as the olive oil is hot, add the coated chicken breasts and sauté, turning once, until they are golden brown on both sides, 3 ½ to 4 minutes per side. Remove the chicken to a plate and cover loosely to keep warm.

5. RETURN THE SAUTÉ PAN to medium-high heat. Add 2 tablespoons of the butter and the shallot and stir. Add the mushrooms and sauté until they begin to give up their juices, 3 to 5 minutes.

6. ADD THE SPINACH and sauté, stirring, until just wilted, 30 to 60 seconds. Do not overcook. Spoon the mushrooms and spinach onto a platter. Arrange the chicken breasts on top.

7. RETURN THE PAN to the heat again. Pour in the ⅓ cup wine and bring to a boil, scraping up all the brown bits from the bottom with a wooden spoon. Boil until the wine is reduced to 1 tablespoon. Add the stock and lemon juice and boil until reduced by half. Remove from the heat and stir in the remaining butter and the tarragon. Pour over the chicken and serve at once.

"By the following summer, we were growing green beans, zucchini, summer squash, peas, peppers, Boston Bibb lettuce, and the *treasured tomatoes*."

Vegetables *and* Sides

Ethel Kennedy's summer house

Sautéed Asparagus

SERVES 4

WHILE I CALL THIS SAUTÉED, actually the asparagus are briefly boiled first and then finished over a flame in a touch of butter to glaze them. This two-step process makes service very easy, because you can blanch the asparagus hours in advance and rewarm them in the butter just before serving.

The skin of the asparagus is fibrous, so classically trained chefs always peel it, leaving the tender tips intact. It also makes for a very attractive presentation. However, if you wish to skip this step, you may, especially if the asparagus are not very thick.

1 pound asparagus spears
1 tablespoon butter
Salt and freshly ground pepper

1. TRIM OFF THE BOTTOMS of the asparagus, leaving the spears about 5 inches long. Using a swivel-bladed vegetable peeler, shave the skin off the lower 3 inches of the asparagus.

2. BRING ABOUT A QUART of salted water to a boil. Add the asparagus to the boiling water and cook until the tips are bright green and the spears are just tender, 3 to 4 minutes.

3. DRAIN IMMEDIATELY and rinse under cold running water; drain well. (The asparagus can be prepared to this point up to 3 hours in advance.)

4. MELT THE BUTTER in a large skillet over medium-high heat. Add the asparagus and toss gently until hot. Season with salt and pepper and serve.

Braised Cabbage

SERVES 6

CABBAGE IS AN UNDERUTILIZED VEGETABLE in the United States. Most people only think of cabbage in cole slaw. In fact, it is a subtle and versatile accompaniment when lightly cooked…especially when paired with bacon and vinegar, as it is here.

3 slices of bacon, diced

1 small onion, thinly sliced

2 pounds green cabbage, shredded into ¼-inch strips

1 tablespoon sugar

½ cup chicken stock

2 tablespoons cider vinegar

3 tablespoons butter

Salt and freshly ground pepper

1. IN A LARGE HEAVY SKILLET, fry the bacon over medium-high heat until beginning to brown but not yet crisp, about 3 minutes. Add the onion and cook, stirring occasionally, until softened and translucent, about 3 minutes longer.

2. ADD THE CABBAGE and sugar. Cover, reduce the heat to medium, and cook, stirring occasionally, until the cabbage is just tender, 5 to 7 minutes.

3. ADD THE CHICKEN STOCK and boil uncovered until the liquid is reduced to a syrup, about 4 minutes.

4. STIR IN THE VINEGAR and butter. Season with salt and pepper to taste.

Citrus-Glazed Carrots

SERVES 4 TO 6

THE SWEETNESS OF FRESH ORANGE and sprightliness of lemon juice play off the natural sweetness of the carrots, amplified here with some extra sugar, to create a vegetable dish the kids will beg for. I often served these at Thanksgiving dinner at the Compound.

1 cup fresh orange juice
1 tablespoon grated orange zest
1 tablespoon lemon juice
¼ to ⅓ cup sugar, to taste
1 pound carrots, peeled and cut on an angle into oval slices

1. IN A NONREACTIVE MEDIUM SAUCEPAN, combine the orange juice, orange zest, lemon juice, and sugar. Boil until reduced to about ⅔ cup of slightly thickened syrup, about 3 minutes. Remove from the heat.

2. IN A LARGE SAUCEPAN of boiling water, cook the carrots until tender, 4 to 5 minutes. Drain into a colander and rinse under cold running water to stop the cooking; drain well. (Both the carrots and glaze can be prepared several hours in advance.)

3. WHEN YOU'RE READY to serve, reheat the glaze. Add the carrots and toss gently to coat. Cook over medium-low heat, stirring once or twice, until hot.

Sautéed Green Beans with Morels

SERVES 4 TO 6

MORELS ARE A WONDERFUL SPRINGTIME MUSHROOM with a deep, smoky flavor. If you cannot get them fresh and at other times of the year, reconstituted dried make a good substitute.

¾ pound green beans, trimmed

2 tablespoons olive oil

1 small onion, chopped

4 ounces fresh or reconstituted dried morels, or substitute fresh shiitakes

2 garlic cloves, crushed through a press

2 tablespoons butter

Salt and freshly ground pepper

1. IN LARGE SAUCEPAN of boiling salted water, cook the green beans until tender, 4 to 5 minutes. Remove and strain. Shock the beans by placing immediately into a bowl filled with ice and cold water. This will keep the beans bright green. When the beans are cold, remove from the water.

2. IN A HEAVY SAUTÉ PAN or large skillet, heat the olive oil over medium heat, add the onion and cook until translucent, then add the morels and garlic. Cook until tender, about 3 to 4 minutes.

3. ADD THE COLD GREEN BEANS and cook until the beans are warmed through, about 3 minutes. Add the butter, toss, and season with salt and pepper to taste.

A GARDEN BY THE SEA

Tomatoes, fresh vegetables, and seafood—always the most popular foods on the Compound, next to homemade chocolate chip cookies. During my first several years on the job, I bought everything from local farmers, grocers, and fish markets, with the exception of many herbs, which I grew in big wine barrels that had been cut in half. They soaked up the sun in back of the house, on a strip of land near the swimming pool and gave off their green scents to passersby of basil, parsley, dill, oregano, chives, and rosemary. I put these herbs into everything from scrambled eggs to soups, where they added flavors that were both subtle and intense at the same time.

One July morning, as I plucked chives and sprigs of rosemary from my wine barrels, the Senator stopped to watch. I thought he was just admiring the plantings and imagining how they might taste if sautéed in butter and garlic over a plate of fresh shellfish.

"Neil," he said, "why don't we start a garden, a real vegetable garden?"

What a great idea, I thought, realizing immediately that beefsteak tomatoes would have to be a key crop. The Senator was crazy about them. For lunches and dinners, I often served them sliced and shingled on a separate plate, with a splash of vinaigrette, whether the main course was grilled fish or Caesar salad. The Senator even liked tomatoes with his breakfast. I'd sauté them sliced in butter and serve them with his eggs.

I got started on the garden right away, consulting the groundskeeper and the gardeners about where to put it and when to begin. Together we found a small piece of land that would get plenty of sunlight, about twenty feet by twenty, between the swimming pool and the tennis court. We built a wire fence around it, to keep out animals, and worked step by step through the year. By the following summer, we were growing green beans, zucchini, summer squash, peas, peppers, Boston Bibb lettuce, and the treasured tomatoes. Most of the crop were juicy beefsteaks, but I also planted plum tomatoes we used mostly for sauces and salsas. I haven't been back to visit in some years, but it's nice to think the little garden by the sea is still there.

"Neil," he said, "why don't we start a garden, a real vegetable garden?"

Fresh Peas Française

SERVES 4 TO 6

PEAS ARE ONE OF THE VEGETABLES I grew in my little summer garden next to the swimming pool. They are one of the earlier vegetables, and the Senator in particular loved them. Besides making fresh pea soup I really like using them in this classic vegetable dish. The saltiness of the bacon provides a really nice counterpoint to the sweetness of the peas, and the romaine adds moisture and color.

You'll need about 2 pounds in the pod to end up with 2 cups shelled. These days, many supermarkets and greengrocers sell them already shelled, but then you miss some of the summer fun.

2 cups freshly shelled peas
3 strips of thickly sliced bacon
2 tablespoons butter
4 large outer romaine leaves, cut crosswise into thin strips
Salt and freshly ground pepper

1. BRING 2 QUARTS of lightly salted water to a boil. Add the peas and cook until tender, 4 to 5 minutes. Drain the peas and rinse well under cold running water; this will keep their color bright green.

2. IN A LARGE SAUTÉ PAN or deep skillet, cook the bacon over medium heat, turning, until it is lightly browned but not completely crisp, about 5 minutes. Drain on paper towels. Pour the fat out of the pan. Cut the bacon into fairly fine dice or coarsely chop it.

3. IN THE SAME SKILLET, melt the butter over medium heat. Add the lettuce and cook, tossing, until the lettuce starts to wilt, 2 to 3 minutes. Add the peas and diced bacon. Cook, tossing gently, until the peas are hot, about 2 minutes longer. Season with salt and pepper to taste. Serve at once.

Chef's Note: In a pinch—or in winter—you can substitute frozen baby peas, though the taste will not be as garden fresh. If you use these, dump the still-frozen peas into the water and cook for 1 to 2 minutes only.

Pan-Fried Plantains

SERVES 4 PEOPLE

PLANTAINS ARE ALMOST COMPLETELY BLACK when they're ripe, but you usually have to buy them when they are yellow and let them hang out in a basket in the kitchen for a few days to ripen. While they look like a banana, they are actually more of a sweet starchy vegetable, and I particularly like to serve them with pork.

2 ripe plantains, peeled
1 tablespoon butter
1 tablespoon brown sugar
¼ teaspoon ground cinnamon

1. CUT THE PLANTAINS crosswise in half and then lengthwise in half to quarter them.

2. MELT THE BUTTER in a large skillet over medium heat. Add the plantains and cook, turning, until lightly browned all over, 4 to 5 minutes.

3. SPRINKLE THE BROWN sugar and cinnamon over the plantains and cook until the sugar dissolves.

Andouille Mashed Potatoes

SERVES 4 TO 6

BEING IRISH MYSELF, I TEND to make my mashed potato portions generous, because a whole generation in Ireland lived off of them. Today, no one goes hungry, but everyone eats mountains of my mashed potatoes. Leftovers make great potato cakes.

6 large baking potatoes (10 to 12 ounces each), peeled and cut into chunks

5 tablespoons butter

½ cup milk

Salt and freshly ground pepper

4 ounces andouille sausage, chopped

Chopped parsley, for garnish

1. IN A LARGE SAUCEPAN of boiling salted water, cook the potatoes until soft, 12 to 15 minutes. Drain into a colander.

2. WHILE THE POTATOES are cooking, heat the milk and 4 tablespoons of the butter. Season with ½ teaspoon salt and ⅛ teaspoon pepper.

3. RETURN THE POTATOES to the pot and mash with a wire potato masher or put through a ricer. Whisk in the hot milk and butter. Continue to beat until the potatoes are smooth.

4. MELT 1 TABLESPOON BUTTER in a small skillet over medium-high heat. Add the andouille sausage and cook, stirring constantly, until hot, about 2 mintues.

5. NOW ADD the andouille sausage to the mashed potates and blend well. Serve while hot with the chopped parsley sprinkled on top.

Potatoes au Gratin

SERVES 4 TO 6

POTATOES ARE ONE OF THE WORLD'S GREAT INGREDIENTS. Almost everyone loves them, and the Kennedys were no exception. Potatoes, after all, are something of an Irish treasure. Don't forget, it was a blight of this crop that led to the terrible famine that forced so many Irish people to emigrate to the United States.

My version of "au gratin potatoes" has no heavy sauce. Instead, sliced potatoes are layered with a little cream and a lot of freshly grated imported Parmesan cheese, and topped with melted butter, which seeps through the entire dish while it bakes. You could substitute Gruyère or a good sharp Cheddar cheese, if you prefer. Whichever you choose, sprigs of fresh herbs are nice as a colorful garnish.

3 large Idaho potatoes (about 12 ounces each)
⅓ cup heavy cream
1 cup freshly grated Parmesan cheese
Salt and freshly ground pepper
4 tablespoons butter, melted

1. PREHEAT THE OVEN to 350 degrees F. Peel the potatoes. Using a mandolin or Japanese vegetable slicer, cut the potatoes into paper-thin rounds.

2. BUTTER a 9-inch pie pan. Beginning at the outer edge, arrange the potatoes in overlapping slices, forming concentric circles that completely cover the bottom of the pan.

3. NOW DRIZZLE about 1 tablespoon of heavy cream over the potatoes. Then sprinkle about 3 tablespoons of the Parmesan cheese over this layer of potatoes. Season with salt and pepper to taste. Repeat this layering to use all the potatoes and fill the pie pan. Drizzle the melted butter evenly over the top.

4. BAKE UNCOVERED for 40 to 45 minutes, or until the potatoes are tender and the top is golden brown. Remove from the oven and let stand for 5 to 10 minutes so the dish has a chance to set up. Then place a large round platter on top and invert to unmold. Cut into wedges to serve.

Chef's Note: For an informal dinner, you can make this dish in a black cast-iron skillet or in a casserole and serve right out of the pan.

Traditional Irish Champ

SERVES 4 TO 6

THIS IS AN UPSCALE VERSION OF MASHED POTATOES, which is loaded with butter. All the Kennedys loved it. Russet baking potatoes, unlike waxy boiling potatoes like Yukon Gold or Red Bliss, are mealy and fall apart when cooked. That's why they are the potato of choice for a smooth mash like this one.

2 pounds baking potatoes, peeled and cut into 1½-inch chunks
1½ sticks (6 ounces) butter, cut into 6 pieces
1½ cups milk
6 scallions, finely chopped
Salt and freshly ground pepper

1. BRING A LARGE pot of salted water to a boil. Add the potatoes and cook until they are soft when pierced with a fork, 10 to 15 minutes. Drain into a colander.

2. WHILE THE POTATOES are cooking, place the butter, milk, and scallions in a small saucepan. Set over medium-low heat until the butter melts and the milk is hot. Remove from the heat.

3. EITHER PUT the potatoes through a ricer or mash with a wire potato masher. Whisk in the hot milk, butter, and scallions until the potatoes are light and smooth. Season with salt and freshly ground pepper to taste.

Sideboard in Rose Kennedy's dining room.

Potato Cakes with Tomato and Basil

SERVES 4

I ALWAYS MADE THESE WHEN I HAD leftover mashed potatoes. But, then, I was cooking for a very large family. Here I've included making the mashed potatoes from scratch.

2 large baking potatoes (10 to 12 ounces each), peeled and quartered

¼ cup finely chopped onion

2 tablespoons butter

Salt and freshly ground pepper

3 eggs

3 tablespoons tomato sauce

1 tablespoon chopped fresh basil

¼ cup shredded Parmesan cheese

¼ cup milk

¾ cup all-purpose flour

¾ cup seasoned bread crumbs

Vegetable oil, for frying

1. IN A MEDIUM SAUCEPAN of boiling salted water, cook the potatoes until tender when pierced with a fork, 10 to 15 minutes. Drain well; transfer to a mixing bowl.

2. WHILE THE POTATOES are cooking, in a small skillet, cook the onion in the butter over medium heat until it turns golden, about 7 minutes.

3. SCRAPE THE ONION with all the butter clinging to the pan into the bowl with the potatoes. Mash with a potato masher, then whisk until nice and smooth. Season with salt and pepper taste.

4. ADD 1 OF THE EGGS and whisk until well blended. Mix in the tomato sauce, basil, and Parmesan cheese. Spread out the mashed potato mixture on a baking sheet and refrigerate until cold and set, about 1 hour. (The potato mixture can be prepared up to a day in advance.)

5. SHAPE THE MASHED POTATOES into 4 patties ½ to ¾ inch thick. In a wide shallow bowl, beat the remaining 2 eggs with the milk to make an egg wash. Dust the potato patties with the flour, dip in the egg wash, and then dredge in the bread crumbs to coat completely.

6. IN A DEEP FRYER or large heavy saucepan, heat at least 1½ inches of oil to 375 degrees F. Add the potato cakes, in two batches if necessary, and fry until hot and golden brown, 3 to 4 minutes.

Honey-Pecan Sweet Potatoes

SERVES 6

NO ONE CAN RESIST THESE STREUSEL-TOPPED mashed sweets. It's a perfect recipe to double, or even triple, for Thanksgiving.

4 large sweet potatoes, peeled and cut into 6 or 8 chunks each
6 tablespoons butter
¾ cup packed light brown sugar
½ teaspoon ground cinnamon
Pinch of grated nutmeg
½ teaspoon vanilla extract
¼ cup all-purpose flour
3 tablespoons honey
½ cup chopped pecans

1. PREHEAT THE OVEN to 350 degrees F.

2. IN A MEDIUM POT bring 2 quarts water to a boil, add the sweet potatoes and cook for 15 to 20 minutes, or until soft. Drain into a colander.

3. RETURN THE SWEET POTATOES to the pot, add 2 tablespoons of the butter, and mash with a potato masher or electric hand mixer. Add ¼ cup of the brown sugar, the cinnamon, nutmeg, and vanilla. Mix to blend well. Transfer the sweet potatoes to a buttered 1½- to 2-quart casserole or baking dish.

4. IN A MEDIUM BOWL prepare the topping by blending the remaining ½ cup brown sugar with the flour. Melt the remaining 4 tablespoons butter and stir in the honey. Scrape this mixture onto the brown sugar and flour, add the pecans, and mix well.

5. SPREAD THIS TOPPING over the sweet potatoes as evenly as you can. (The recipe can be prepared to this point up to a day in advance. Cover with foil and refrigerate.)

6. TO FINISH, PREHEAT the oven to 350 degrees F. Bake the sweet potato casserole for about 25 to 35 minutes, until the potatoes are piping hot and the topping is lightly browned and crisp.

Honeyed Butternut Squash

SERVES 4 TO 6

MANY SUPERMARKETS SELL SQUASH already peeled and cut up. If you see these chunks in the produce section, they are a great time saver, especially if you're cooking an entire holiday meal.

2 small butternut squash, peeled, seeded, and cut into chunks

4 tablespoons butter, cut up

¼ cup packed brown sugar

2 tablespoons honey

Salt and freshly ground pepper

1. BRING 2 QUARTS water to a boil in a large saucepan over high heat. Then add the cut-up butternut squash. Boil for about 4 minutes to jump-start the cooking, then reduce the heat to medium and cook for 20 minutes, or until the squash is tender.

2. STRAIN INTO A COLANDER to remove as much liquid as possible. Then return to the pot. With a potato masher or electric hand mixer, mash the sweet potatoes. Add the butter, brown sugar, and honey and mix well. Season with salt and freshly ground pepper to taste.

Swiss Chard with Fresh Shiitake Mushrooms and Sweet Pepper

4 TO 6 SERVINGS

COLORFUL AND LIGHT, SWISS CHARD is one of those nice green leafy vegetables that goes well with just about anything: chicken, beef, lamb, or pork...even fish. Save the white stems for soup, if you like.

1 bunch of Swiss chard, green leaves only
3 tablespoons extra virgin olive oil
1 medium onion, chopped
10 to 12 fresh shiitake mushrooms, stems removed, caps sliced
1 small red bell pepper, cut into ½-inch dice
1 tablespoon lemon juice
Salt and freshly ground pepper

1. RINSE THE SWISS CHARD leaves well; drain. Cut lengthwise in half, then crosswise into ½- to 1-inch strips.

2. IN A LARGE SKILLET, heat 2 tablespoons of the olive oil over medium-high heat. Add the onion and sauté until it is softened and just beginning to color, 4 to 5 minutes. Add the shiitake mushrooms and red bell pepper and sauté for 3 minutes longer.

3. ADD THE SWISS CHARD pieces to the skillet in bunches, stirring or tossing with tongs as they wilt. Reduce the heat to medium and continue to cook, stirring, until the chard is tender, 3 to 5 minutes. Strain off any excess liquid.

4. ADD THE REMAINING 1 tablespoon olive oil and the lemon juice and toss with the vegetables. Season with salt and pepper to taste.

Mashed Buttered Turnips

SERVES 4

THIS SIMPLE BUT TRADITIONAL DISH was always part of the Thanksgiving menu, which included all the trimmings.

4 medium turnips, peeled and quartered
5 tablespoons butter, melted
1½ teaspoons chopped parsley
½ teaspoon salt
¼ teaspoon freshly ground pepper

1. BRING A LARGE SAUCEPAN of salted water to a boil. Add the turnips and cook for 20 to 25 minutes, or until tender. Drain into a colander.

2. RETURN THE TURNIPS to the pot and mash with a potato masher until smooth. Whisk in the melted butter, parsley, salt, and pepper. Turn into a warmed dish and serve hot.

Thanksgiving Menu at the Compound

Hot Mulled Cider
Assorted Sweet Breads with Marmalade Butter

Assorted Relishes

Fall Greens with Toasted Pumpkin Seeds

Oven-Roasted Vermont Turkey
Sage Stuffing
Honey-Pecan Sweet Potatoes
Mashed Potatoes
Butternut Squash
Acorn Squash
Mashed Buttered Turnips
Glazed Carrots
Buttered Peas

Apple Pie
Pumpkin Pie

Rice Pilaf with Vegetables

SERVES 4 TO 6

PILAF SIMPLY MEANS THE RICE has been cooked in butter or oil with aromatics and sometimes vegetables before the stock or water is added. Here I use carrots and green beans for color and mushrooms for extra flavor. It's a fine side dish to serve with almost any meat, poultry, or fish.

3 tablespoons butter
¼ cup finely chopped onion
¼ cup finely diced (¼ inch) carrots
¼ cup finely diced (¼ inch) mushrooms
¼ cup thinly sliced (¼ inch) green beans
Salt and freshly ground pepper
1½ cups basmati rice
1 bay leaf
3 cups chicken stock

1. IN A MEDIUM SAUCEPAN, melt the butter over medium heat. Add the onion and cook for 2 minutes. Add the carrots, mushrooms, and green beans and cook, stirring occasionally, until the vegetables are slightly softened, 3 to 4 minutes. Season lightly with salt and pepper.

2. ADD THE RICE and stir to coat with the butter and mix with the vegetables. Add the bay leaf. Pour in the stock and bring to a simmer. Cover, reduce the heat to low, and cook until the liquid is absorbed and the rice is tender, 12 to 15 minutes.

Chef's Note: There are over 100,000 varieties of rice in the world. Basmati rice is considered to be one of the world's best because of its sweet, nutty flavor. It has been grown in the Himalayan mountain ranges for centuries, though now it is cultivated all over the world. When making a rice pilaf, I prefer using Basmati because of its wonderful natural flavor. Converted rice is foolproof if you need the insurance, meaning it won't stick and is very hard to overcook, but it lacks the flavor and texture of basmati, jasmine, and other unprocessed varieties.

Chive Rice Cakes

4 TO 6 SERVINGS

BASMATI RICE IS MY FAVORITE BECAUSE it is tender and has a really nice nutty taste. Plus, it cooks a bit faster than other varieties. You can, however, use any long-grain white rice you have on hand here. Think of this recipe any time you have leftovers; you need about 3 cups to form the cakes.

2 cups chicken stock
1 cup basmati rice
1 egg
½ teaspoon salt
¼ teaspoon freshly ground pepper
1 tablespoon minced fresh chives
2 tablespoons olive oil

1. IN A SMALL SAUCEPAN, bring the stock to a boil. Add the rice, reduce the heat to low, cover, and cook until the liquid is absorbed and the rice is tender, about 15 minutes. Spread out the rice on a baking sheet and let cool.

2. PREHEAT THE OVEN to 350 degrees F. In a medium bowl, beat the egg lightly with the salt and pepper. Add the rice and chives and mix well. Shape the mixture into round cakes about 2½ inches in diameter and about ½ inch thick.

3. HEAT THE OIL in a large skillet over medium heat. Add the rice cakes and cook until lightly browned on both sides and hot throughout, about 3 minutes on each side.

Saffron Risotto

4 SERVINGS

ACTUALLY, THERE'S ONLY A PINCH OF SAFFRON in this rice dish, but it's enough to add a pleasingly subtle flavor and a hint of yellow color. This is the classic "*risotto Milanese*" traditionally served with *osso buco*. I like it with almost any veal or chicken dish.

4 tablespoons butter
½ cup finely chopped onion
1 cup Arborio rice
Pinch of saffron threads
4 cups chicken stock
1 cup grated Parmesan cheese
Salt and freshly ground pepper

1. IN A HEAVY MEDIUM SAUCEPAN, melt 2 tablespoons of the butter over medium heat. Add the onion and cook, stirring occasionally, until it is softened and translucent, 3 to 5 minutes. Add the rice and cook, stirring, for 2 to 3 minutes, until the grains of rice look opaque. Stir in the saffron.

2. NOW ADD ¾ cup of the chicken stock and cook, stirring often, until the stock is absorbed. Add another ¾ cup stock and cook in the same way. If the liquid evaporates too quickly, reduce the heat slightly. Continue to cook, adding the stock gradually and stirring often, until the rice is plumped but still slightly firm in the center, and the stock has formed a creamy sauce, 18 to 22 minutes.

3. REMOVE FROM THE HEAT and add the remaining 2 tablespoons butter. Stir until melted and evenly incorporated. Stir in the Parmesan cheese. Season with salt and pepper to taste and serve immediately.

"Most days, I would fill up several coolers with boat lunches that were already prepared—lobster and tuna salads, thermoses of clam and corn chowder, roast chickens, potato salad and cole slaw—and drive them several blocks to the Hyannis Port harbor."

Salads *of* All Kinds

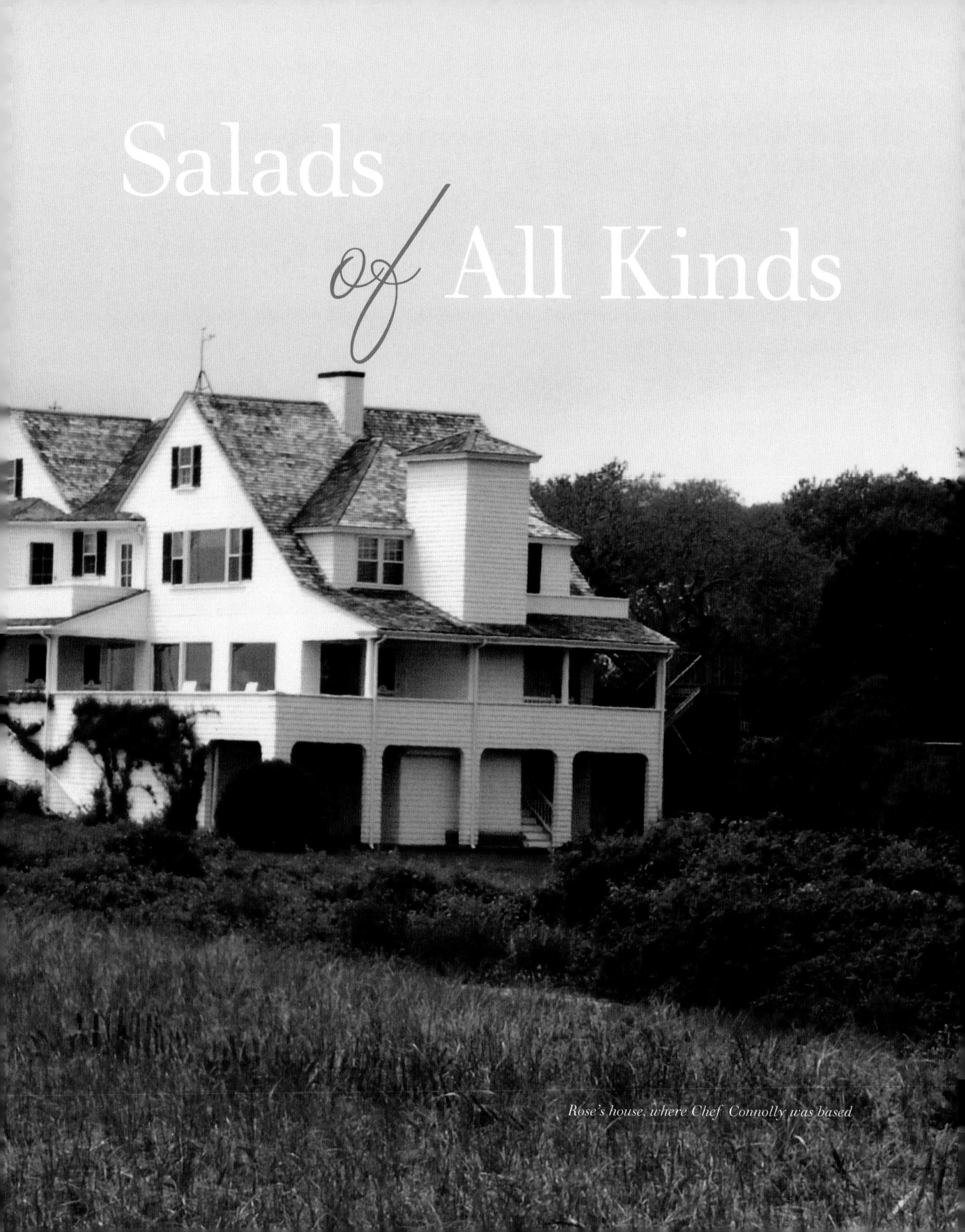

Rose's house, where Chef Connolly was based

Baby Field Greens with Poached Pears and Stilton Cheese

SERVES 4

WHILE MANY PEOPLE SERVE RAW PEARS on a salad like this, I poach them for several reasons: the brief cooking highlights their flavor, softens them slightly, and most importantly, sets their color so they will not turn brown.

1 cup dry white wine
2 cups sugar
2 Bartlett pears, halved, cored and peeled
6 cups of lightly packed baby greens (10 to 12 ounces)
⅓ cup walnut oil
3 tablespoons balsamic vinegar
Salt and freshly ground pepper
6 tablespoons crumbled Stilton, Gorgonzola, or Roquefort cheese
¼ cup chopped toasted walnuts

1. IN A WIDE SAUCEPAN, combine the wine, sugar, and 2 cups of water. Bring to a boil over medium-high heat, stirring to dissolve the sugar. Reduce the heat to a bare simmer.

2. ADD THE PEAR halves and poach them for 10 minutes, or until just tender. Turn them carefully about halfway through so they cook evenly. Use a slotted spoon to transfer the pears to a dish, let cool, then cover and refrigerate until chilled, at least 2 hours or overnight. (The pear syrup can be reserved for poaching other fruit.)

3. IN A SALAD BOWL, combine the baby field greens with the walnut oil, balsamic vinegar, and salt and pepper to taste. Toss the salad to mix well.

4. DIVIDE THE SALAD among 4 plates. Cut the cold pear halves into wedges and fan out on top. Sprinkle the cheese and walnuts on top.

Chef's Note: Toasting of the walnuts is optional, but it really does deepen their flavor. You can brown them lightly in a 350 degree F oven for 7 to 10 minutes, toast them in a dry skillet for 3 or 4 minutes, or in a microwave oven on High for 30 to 60 seconds.

Classic Caesar Salad

SERVES 4

CAESAR SALAD IS JUST ABOUT EVERYONE'S FAVORITE. A few people think they don't like anchovies, but Caesar salad without anchovies is like a hot fudge sundae without the chocolate sauce. Just in case, I put them on top for garnish, so picky eaters can pull them off. For the Kennedys, I made the presentation of this salad special by serving it in a Parmesan cup. If you wish to do the same, I've included the easy directions on page 164.

1 large head of romaine lettuce
1 garlic clove, cut in half
1 or 2 organic eggs, boiled for exactly 1½ minutes
½ cup extra virgin olive oil
3 tablespoons fresh lemon juice
Salt and freshly cracked black pepper
½ cup shredded imported Parmesan cheese
½ cup croutons
8 flat anchovy fillets

1. SEPARATE THE ROMAINE LEAVES. Rinse in a bowl of cold water, tear them into large bite-size pieces, and spin dry.

2. RUB THE BOTTOM AND SIDES of a large wooden bowl with the cut sides of the garlic. Discard the garlic. Crack the eggs into the bowl and whisk to blend. Whisk in the olive oil and lemon juice. Season with salt and pepper to taste.

3. ADD THE LETTUCE TO THE dressing in the salad bowl and toss to coat. Add the cheese and croutons and toss lightly to mix. Divide among 4 salad plates or arrange in Parmesan Cups (page 164). Garnish each serving with an extra grind of pepper and 2 anchovy fillets. Serve at once.

Parmesan Cup for Caesar Salad

MAKES 4

TO MAKE FORMING THESE EASY, you might want to bake them in two batches, so you have time to mold each cup before the cheese hardens.

2 cups shredded Parmesan cheese, about 8 ounces

1. PREHEAT THE OVEN to 375 degrees F. Line 2 baking sheets or cookie sheets with parchment or waxed paper. Trace two 6-inch rounds on each, leaving at least 2 inches between them.

2. FILL IN THE CIRCLES with the cheese, spreading it as evenly as possible. Bake for 4 to 5 minutes, or until golden brown.

3. QUICKLY, WHILE THE CHEESE IS SOFT, use a wide spatula to transfer the rounds, one at time to an inverted wide-bottomed bowl 3 to 4 inches in diameter. Make sure you do this right away, or the cheese will become too brittle to mold. Gently press the hot cheese onto the bowl; it will set up almost immediately. Slip the cheese cup off the bowl and let it cool and harden completely before using.

Chicken Salad with Red and Green Grapes

4 TO 6 SERVINGS

Poaching chicken breasts is very easy, and you end up with both the meat of the chicken and a simple broth that makes a fine base for soups and sauces. Keep in mind, though, that this delightful luncheon salad can be made with any form of cooked chicken—poached, roast, or torn off a rotisserie chicken, as long as you end up with 3 cups.

1 pound skinless, boneless chicken breasts
3 tablespoons finely chopped white onion
3 tablespoons finely diced celery
1 teaspoon minced fresh tarragon or ½ teaspoon dried
½ cup mayonnaise
Salt and freshly ground pepper
8 red seedless grapes, cut in half
8 green seedless grapes, cut in half

1. PUT THE CHICKEN BREASTS in a medium saucepan and cover with salted water. Bring to a simmer over medium-low heat and poach the chicken until it is white through to the center but still moist and juicy, about 10 minutes. Do not let the liquid come to a boil, or the meat will toughen. Chill in the refrigerator for at least 1 hour. (The chicken can be poached a day or two in advance.)

2. TRIM OFF ANY BITS OF FAT and gristle from the chicken breasts. Cut the meat into generous bite-size chunks.

3. IN A MIXING BOWL, combine the diced chicken with the onion, celery, tarragon, and mayonnaise. Toss to mix well. Season with salt and pepper to taste. Add the grapes and toss lightly to distribute them evenly. Cover and refrigerate the salad until ready to serve.

Belgian Endive Salad with Apples, Cucumber, and Cashews

SERVES 4

THE SWEETNESS OF APPLE AND RICHNESS OF CASHEWS both tame the pleasing bitterness of the endive and watercress in this refreshing salad. I like the way the raspberry vinaigrette complements the flavors and adds color, but if you prefer, you could dress the salad simply with your favorite vinegar and extra virgin olive oil.

2 heads of Belgian endive, separated into individual leaves
1 large cucumber, peeled, seeded, and cut into thin julienne strips
2 Granny Smith apples, cored, and cut into thin julienne strips
½ cup toasted cashews
¾ cup Raspberry Vinaigrette (recipe page 170)
1 small bunch of watercress, tough stems removed

1. FAN OUT the endive leaves on 4 chilled plates.

2. IN A MEDIUM BOWL, combine the cucumber, apples, and cashews. Add ⅓ cup of the vinaigrette and toss to coat. Mound equal portions of the salad in the center of the endive leaves.

3. GARNISH EACH PLATE with a small bouquet of watercress. Pass more of the raspberry vinaigrette on the side.

Spring Roll Salad with Green Apple-Mango Vinaigrette

4 SERVINGS

RICE PAPER WRAPPERS, USUALLY THAI or Vietnamese, are available in Asian markets or the Southeast Asian section of your supermarket. They need no cooking, just a brief dip in warm water to soften, which makes them ideal for a summer dish.

1 cup shredded arugula
1 cup shredded bok choy (white stems only)
1 cup shredded Napa cabbage
1 small mango, peeled, pitted and cut into thin julienne strips
1 Granny Smith apple, peeled, cored and cut into thin julienne strips
½ red bell pepper, seeded and cut into thin julienne strips
½ medium red onion, thinly sliced
4 round sheets of rice paper, about 8 inches in diameter
Green Apple-Mango Vinaigrette (recipe follows)
1 small bunch of pea shoots or sprouts
4 fresh chives (optional)

1. PREPARE ALL YOUR VEGETABLES and fruits first. Combine the shredded arugula, bok choy, Napa cabbage, mango, apple, bell pepper, and red onion. Toss to mix well.

2. ONE AT A TIME, soak a rice paper wrapper in a bowl of warm water just until soft and pliable, 20 to 30 seconds. Immediately remove from the water and place flat on your work surface. Spoon one fourth of the salad mixture into the center. Roll the bottom up, fold in the sides, and roll up snuggly like an egg roll. (The filled wrappers can be rolled up to 2 hours in advance, wrapped, and refrigerated.

3. TO FINISH THE SALAD, cut each spring roll crosswise in half on an angle. Arrange on plates and drizzle a couple of tablespoons of apple-mango vinaigrette over each serving. Pass the remainder on the side. Garnish each plate with pea tendrils and chives, if you like.

Green Apple-Mango Vinaigrette

MAKES ABOUT 1 CUP

½ cup vegetable oil
¼ cup rice vinegar
2 tablespoons sugar
2 tablespoons tamari
½ Granny Smith apple, peeled, cored, finely diced
½ ripe mango, cut off the pit and finely diced

WHISK TOGETHER the oil, vinegar, sugar, and tamari until the sugar dissolves. Stir in the apple and mango. Give the dressing a stir just before using it.

Raspberry Vinaigrette

MAKES ABOUT 1½ CUPS

THIS WILL MAKE ABOUT TWICE as much dressing as you need. I suggest passing the extra on the side or refrigerate in a covered jar to use in another salad. It will keep well for up to 5 days.

1 cup fresh or frozen raspberries
⅓ cup vegetable oil
3 tablespoons olive oil
¼ cup red wine vinegar
2 tablespoons sugar
Salt and freshly ground pepper

IN A BLENDER or food processor, combine the raspberries, vegetable oil, olive oil, vinegar, and sugar. Puree until smooth. Season the dressing with salt and pepper. Cover and refrigerate until ready to use.

MOVABLE FEASTS ABOARD THE MYA

Sailing comes almost as naturally to the Kennedys as politics does. From the family's earliest days in Hyannis, in 1926, even the youngest have been avid sailors, encouraged by their ambitious parents to be competitive, competent, and self-possessed. In good times and difficult times, they take to the water for pleasure, sport, relaxation, and solace. One by one, as the smallest of them grow up, they learn essential lessons about safety and boating. The family lore is that no one is allowed to sail until he or she has been thrown overboard and learns first-hand the power of the ocean.

In a family as large and close knit as this is, lessons are handed down as much from sibling to sibling as they are from parent to child. In 1979, when Senator Kennedy helped dedicate the John F. Kennedy Library in Boston, he spoke movingly about the influence of the beloved brother who was fourteen years his senior: "He taught me to ride a bicycle, to throw a forward pass, and to sail against the wind…He might have sailed with Magellan, navigating beyond the charts to the new and better world he sought."

Like most members of the family, the Senator wears many hats—statesman, father, husband, uncle, friend, and generous host—but he cherishes his role as sailor as much as any of them. He sails in every season, not just summer. His 50-foot schooner, the *Mya*, is nearly a member of the family.

In my decade on the Compound, the *Mya* was always a movable feast. Whether the Senator was taking out family members or friends, John Jr. and his wife, Carolyn, or legendary newsman Walter Cronkite, the boat would not set sail until it was stocked with plenty of food and cold drinks.

Sailing comes almost as naturally to the Kennedys as politics does.

Most days, I would fill up several coolers with boat lunches that were already prepared—lobster and tuna salads, thermoses of clam and corn chowder, roast chickens, potato salad, and cole slaw—and drive them several blocks to the Hyannis Port harbor. I'd carry the coolers down the long wooden pier to the

Neil with Irish chef Noel Cullen: Getting ready for a boat lunch on the Mya.

(continued)

MOVABLE FEASTS ABOARD THE MYA *continued*

Senator's speedboat, load everything on it and zip out to the *Mya*, which had to be anchored in deeper water, about 300 feet away. The Senator and crew members would take the coolers from me and set off, whether it was to Nantucket and back for the afternoon or overnight to Martha's Vineyard.

There were a few times when they'd be heading on a long cruise, and I'd get a phone call from the boat—an SOS: They were out of supplies! I'd whip up more lobster salad, a thermos of chowder, then head down to the pier and take off on the speedboat, meeting the *Mya* under sail for an —emergency "refueling." And there were many times I was invited to come along for the trip. I'd bring plenty of food that was already prepared and also the makings for a few dishes that could be put together in a kitchen that rocked and rolled with the sea. It took some time getting used to the unsteady surroundings, and I was always extra careful with a sharp knife. I'd bring vegetables and lettuce from our garden and cut everything right before I served it, to keep it fresh. Shrimp scampi was a favorite boat lunch. It was easy to cook in the limited kitchen on the *Mya*, and it's a dish that has to be served hot off the stove.

"The family lore is that no one is allowed to sail until he or she has been

Once I was finished cooking and serving, the Senator always invited me to stay on deck with him and his guests—and pitch in sailing. I had lived on the Cape for many years and done a bit of boating, but it wasn't until my time on the *Mya* that I really acquired my sea legs and

move, carrying a cooler on my shoulder and going up the rungs of the wooden ladder on the side of the pier. I raised my foot to the next rung—and it wasn't there. I lost my balance, dropped the cooler, and fell backward into the harbor.

It wasn't a long drop, and I wasn't hurt. But I was sopping wet, and so was my

thrown overboard and learns first-hand the power of the ocean."

learned what to do with a mainsail and a jib. It was a great thrill and a pleasure being on the *Mya*—an energizing change of scenery from the kitchen.

Luckily, in my years of cooking at sea, I never had any mishaps with a knife or a hot skillet. But I had one on the pier I'll never forget. One afternoon after the Senator had come in from a sail, he had gone up to the house and I was taking the coolers from the speedboat onto the wooden pier. I had done it hundreds of times, but it was still a delicate

long chef's coat. When I retrieved the cooler and made my way back to the house, the Senator took a startled look at me. "What happened?"

"I missed the last step."

We had a laugh over that. Four years later, after I baked the six-tiered cake for his daughter Kara's wedding, he wrote me a note I'll always cherish, saying that I hadn't missed the bottom step on the day of the wedding, "and then again, you never do."

ABOVE: *Kara Kennedy Allen, Kiki Kennedy, the Senator's son Ted Jr., and the Senator returning from a sail.*
FACING PAGE: *Senator Kennedy's sailboat, the* Mya, *in full sail.*

Lobster Salad with Fresh Fruit

SERVES 4

LOBSTER SALAD WAS A FAVORITE at the compound both for lunches on the boat and for light meals at the house. As you can see from this recipe, I went all out to make the food not only taste delicious, but look striking and beautiful. That's why I use such a colorful assortment of fruit and berries. You can easily make the salad with just one or two varieties of berries and one melon. Just increase the quantities accordingly.

1 pound freshly cooked lobster meat (from the tail, claws, and knuckles)
½ cup mayonnaise, preferably homemade (page 41)
1 teaspoon orange oil or 1 tablespoon freshly squeezed orange juice and 1 teaspoon grated zest
¼ cup finely diced celery
8 blackberries
8 raspberries
8 strawberries, sliced or quartered
1 cup finely diced cantaloupe
1 cup finely diced honeydew melon
4 very thin lengthwise slices of European seedless cucumber
2 cups loosely packed mixed baby field greens (mesclun)
Creamy Grand Marnier Dressing (recipe follows)

1. CUT THE LOBSTER into ½-inch chunks. In a medium bowl, blend the mayonnaise and orange oil or juice and zest. Stir in the celery and onion. Add the lobster and toss gently to coat. Cover and refrigerate the lobster salad for up to 4 hours until ready to serve.

2. COMBINE THE BLACKBERRIES, raspberries, strawberries, cantaloupe, and honeydew. Set the fruit mixture aside.

3. USING A 3½-INCH ROUND pastry cutter or an empty tuna fish can, wrap a ribbon of cucumber around the inside to make a ring. Place the cutter with the cucumber to one side of a dinner plate. Fill with the lobster salad. Gently remove the ring, leaving the cucumber wrapped around the salad. Repeat this 3 more times.

4. ARRANGE A SMALL BOUQUET of field greens next to the round of salad on each plate. Decorate with the mixed fruit. Spoon about 1 tablespoon of the Creamy Grand Marnier Dressing over part of the lobster salad. Pass the remaining dressing on the side.

Creamy Grand Marnier Dressing

MAKES ABOUT 1 CUP

1 cup sour cream
2 tablespoons fresh orange juice
2 tablespoons Grand Marnier
1 tablespoon honey
1 teaspoon grated orange zest
1 teaspoon sugar

COMBINE all the ingredients in a bowl. Whisk until well blended. Cover and refrigerate the Grand Marnier dressing until serving time.

Chef's Note: When I had them, I garnished the top of the salad with a couple of extra small cooked lobster claws as well as spears of fresh chives. You can buy cooked lobster meat, but, of course, the salad is best when made with freshly boiled. It will take 2 lobsters 1 ¼ pounds each to yield about a pound of lobster meat.

Old-Fashioned Potato Salad

SERVES 4 TO 6

AT ROSE'S HOUSE, YOU NEVER KNEW who would be dropping by—some of the kids, neighbors, or other family or friends. I always kept a big bowl of homemade potato salad in the fridge, so anyone who raided the kitchen at any hour would have something to go with the roast chicken or seafood, always on hand, or the deli sandwiches I could whip up on a moment's notice.

2 pounds red-skinned potatoes, preferably organic
1 cup mayonnaise
¼ cup cider vinegar
1 tablespoon chopped parsley
1 teaspoon Dijon mustard
1 cup diced onions
2 hard-boiled eggs, diced
Salt and freshly ground pepper

1. SCRUB THE POTATOES WELL. Cut them in half, leaving the skin on.

2. BOIL THE POTATOES in a large pot of salted water for about 15 minutes, or until tender. Drain and let cool slightly, then refrigerate for about 1 hour, until chilled. Dice the cold potatoes.

3. IN A LARGE BOWL, mix together the mayonnaise, vinegar, parsley, and mustard. Add the diced potatoes, onions, and eggs and toss to mix. Season with salt and pepper to taste. Then refrigerate until ready to use.

Chef's Note: Chilling the cooked potatoes before you dice them allows them time to set up, so they hold their shape when they are cut.

Couscous Salad with Fresh Basil and Feta Cheese

4 TO 6 SERVINGS

SO-CALLED "ISRAELI COUSCOUS" looks like little pearls of pasta. It cooks up into tiny balls that make a wonderful shape for a side salad. This one, loaded with finely diced fresh vegetables, olives, and feta cheese, offers an original alternative to the usual pasta or potato salad. It's also versatile: you can mound it on fresh greens as a vegetarian main-course or add some thinly sliced rings of cooked calamari or shrimp to transform it into a delightful seafood salad.

2 cups Israeli couscous
¼ cup diced red and/or green bell pepper
¼ cup finely diced red onion
¼ cup finely diced celery
¼ cup chopped pitted Kalamata olives
¼ cup diced seeded tomato
3 ounces feta cheese crumbled (about 1 cup)
3 tablespoons shredded fresh basil
2 tablespoons chopped fresh parsley
1 garlic clove, minced
½ cup extra virgin olive oil
¼ cup balsamic vinegar
Salt and freshly ground pepper

1. COOK THE COUSCOUS in a medium saucepan of boiling salted water until *al dente*, tender but still slightly firm, about 10 to 15 minutes. Drain into a colander and rinse under cold running water; drain well. Transfer the couscous to a bowl, cover and refrigerate until chilled, at least 1 hour.

2. PLACE THE CHILLED COUSCOUS in a serving bowl. Add the bell pepper, red onion, celery, olives, tomato, feta cheese, basil, parsley, garlic, olive oil, and vinegar. Toss to mix well. Season with salt and pepper to taste.

Crab Salad

4 TO 6 SERVINGS

IF YOU LIVE NEAR THE SHORE, crab offers a nice alternative to tuna to mound on greens with some hard-cooked egg, sliced tomatoes, and cucumber or to sandwich in a bun. All crabmeat comes precooked, so whether you purchase lump, the premium type, or canned crab, an acceptable alternative for a salad mixture like this, you don't need to do anything to the meat.

1 pound lump or canned crabmeat
¾ cup mayonnaise
3 tablespoons ketchup
1 tablespoon fresh lemon juice
3 tablespoons finely diced celery
2 tablespoons finely diced white onion
Salt and freshly ground pepper

1. IF USING CANNED CRAB, drain and squeeze out as much moisture as possible. With either fresh or canned crab, pick over to remove any bits of shell or cartilage.

2. IN A BOWL, whisk together the mayonnaise, ketchup, and lemon juice. Stir in the celery and white onion.

3. CRUMBLE THE CRAB into fairly small pieces and add to the dressing. If you have lump crabmeat, an occasional larger bit is nice. Toss lightly to mix. Season with salt and pepper to taste. Cover and refrigerate until ready to serve.

Pickled Beet Salad

SERVES 4

Usually I made this salad with red beets, but when yellow were available, it made for a prettier platter. To avoid having them all bleed together, if you have the two kinds of beets, marinate the slices separately before you assemble the salad.

4 medium-size beets, stems trimmed to 1 to 2 inches, well washed

½ cup paper-thin slices of white onion

1 cup cider vinegar

½ cup granulated sugar

1 bunch of fresh pea shoots or watercress

1. COOK THE WHOLE BEETS in a pot of boiling water for 30 to 40 minutes, or until tender. Drain into a colander. When the beets are cool enough to handle, slip off the skins and cut the beets into thin slices.

2. IN A MEDIUM BOWL, combine the vinegar and sugar; stir to dissolve the sugar. Add the beets and onion, cover, and refrigerate for at least 1 hour or up to 5 days, tossing occasionally.

3. TO SERVE, remove the beets and onion slices with a slotted spoon and arrange on a small platter. Garnish with the fresh pea tendrils.

"On sunlit days, with the scent of the salty ocean air, the sound of the waves, and the laughter of children in the distance, it was *as close to perfect* as a Sunday ever comes."

Breakfast *and* Brunch

The Mya *with the Senator at the helm*

Baja Frittata

SERVES 6

MEXICAN BREAKFASTS ARE SOME OF THE BEST in the world, and I borrowed a sampling of those tasty ingredients—spicy chorizo, mild and creamy Monterey Jack cheese, and smoky chipotle chile—to create a big firm omelet that's fine to eat hot, warm, or at room temperature. Any leftovers make a great snack.

12 eggs
1 cup shredded Monterey Jack cheese (3 to 4 ounces)
Splash of Tabasco
½ teaspoon salt
¼ teaspoon freshly ground pepper
2 tablespoons vegetable oil
½ cup diced (⅜-inch) red onion
¼ cup diced (⅜-inch) red bell pepper
¼ cup diced (⅜-inch) green bell pepper
½ cup sliced chorizo, casing removed (2 to 3 ounces)
1 large plum tomato, peeled, seeded, and diced
½ teaspoon minced chipotle chile in adobe sauce

1. PREHEAT THE OVEN to 375 degrees F. Crack the eggs into a large bowl and whisk until fluffy. Add the Monterey Jack cheese, Tabasco, salt, and pepper.

2. HEAT THE OIL in a 12-inch heavy skillet, preferably cast-iron, over medium-high heat. Add the red onion, red and green bell peppers, and the chorizo. Cook, stirring often, until the onion and peppers soften, 4 to 5 minutes.

3. NOW ADD THE TOMATO and chipotle chile and stir well. Pour the egg-cheese mixture into the skillet and immediately transfer to the oven.

4. BAKE, UNCOVERED, for 15 to 20 minutes. When it is done, the frittata will be firm throughout, puffed, and lightly browned on top. Serve cut into wedges right from the skillet.

Kara's Scrambled Eggs and Cheese

SERVES 4

SENATOR KENNEDY'S DAUGHTER KARA was in her teens when I began cooking for the family. I stayed long enough to watch her get married, which moved me greatly. For breakfast, she'd often request these easy eggs. Unlike a lot of youngsters, she liked a real kick of hot sauce, so when I say "a splash" here, feel free to indulge.

8 eggs
1 tablespoon vegetable oil
4 slices of white American cheese, coarsely chopped
Splash of Tabasco, to taste
Salt and freshly ground pepper
1 tablespoon chopped fresh chives

1. CRACK THE EGGS into a bowl and whisk until well blended.

2. HEAT a large seasoned egg pan or nonstick skillet over medium heat with the vegetable oil.

3. WHEN THE OIL is hot but not smoking, pour the beaten eggs into the pan while constantly stirring with a fork.

4. AS SOON AS THE EGGS begin to set, add the American cheese, Tabasco, salt, pepper, and chives, still stirring. When the eggs are fluffy and moist, remove from the heat and serve right away.

Chef's Note: Contrary to what you often read, it's the oil and hot pan that make these scrambled eggs so fluffy, but you must work quickly. The eggs will continue to cook after you remove them from the heat, so always err on the side of undercooking slightly. The eggs should look slightly moist, not dry, when you take them off the heat.

Dublin Shirred Eggs

SERVES 4

SHIRRED EGGS ARE SIMPLY BAKED EGGS, usually done in ramekins and often enhanced with a bit of cream and whatever fresh herb strikes your fancy. For the Senator, I often added a layer of Irish smoked salmon, but you could just as well use prosciutto or even plain ham. For a lovely brunch, begin with melon or mixed fruit and berries and serve with Irish potato cakes on the side.

1 tablespoon butter, at room temperature
¾ cup heavy cream
1 tablespoon chopped fresh chives
Pinch of freshly grated nutmeg
Salt and fresh ground pepper
2 ounces thinly sliced Irish smoked salmon, prosciutto, or ham
4 eggs

1. PREHEAT THE OVEN to 400 degrees F. Grease the inside of four (8-ounce) soufflé dishes or individual ramekins with the butter.

2. IN A SMALL SAUCEPAN, combine the heavy cream, chives, and nutmeg. Season with salt and pepper to taste. Heat until hot.

3. ARRANGE A SLICE of smoked salmon or ham in each buttered dish, folding if necessary to fit. Crack a raw egg into each dish, doing so carefully so the yolk remains intact. Pour 3 tablespoons of the hot chive cream over each egg and place in the oven.

4. BAKE FOR 10 TO 12 MINUTES, or until the white is set but the yolk is still runny, or longer if preferred. Serve at once.

Eggs Chatham-Style with Ham and Mushroom Cream Sauce

SERVES 4

THE FIRST CHOICE OF HAM HERE makes me suspect this must be a Southern version of Eggs Benedict, but somehow it ended up on Cape Cod. Wherever it came from, the dish was very popular in the Kennedy household. Any really flavorful ham, even just baked, will do.

4 slices of flavorful ham, such as smoked Virginia, cut ¼ inch thick
1 teaspoon butter
2 English muffins, split in half and toasted
1 tablespoon vegetable oil
2 tablespoons minced onion
1 cup chopped mushrooms
2 tablespoons dry sherry
1 teaspoon all-purpose flour
1 cup heavy cream
Pinch of freshly grated nutmeg
Salt and freshly ground pepper
½ teaspoon distilled white vinegar
4 eggs

1. HEAT A LARGE HEAVY SKILLET over medium heat. Lightly brown the ham on both sides in the butter, 3 to 4 minutes. Remove from the pan and place a slice on top of each of the 4 toasted English muffin halves. Set aside on individual plates in a warm place, if possible.

2. IN THE SAME SKILLET, heat the vegetable oil. Add the onion and mushrooms and sauté over medium-high heat until the onion is soft and the mushrooms are tender and begin to give up their juices, about 5 minutes.

3. ADD THE SHERRY to the pan and boil, stirring, until almost all the liquid is evaporated. Sprinkle the flour over the mushrooms, reduce the heat to medium, and cook, stirring, for 1 to 2 minutes. Add the heavy cream, nutmeg, ¼ teaspoon salt, and ⅛ teaspoon pepper. Bring to a boil, stirring until the liquid thickens slightly. Reduce the heat and simmer for 5 minutes.

4. MEANWHILE, in a deep skillet or wide saucepan, bring 1 quart of water to a boil. Add the vinegar and reduce the heat to a simmer. Carefully crack the eggs and gently slip into the water. Poach until the whites are firm and the yolks are still runny, 3 to 4 minutes, or longer if desired.

5. PLACE A POACHED EGG on top of each slice of ham. Spoon the mushroom cream sauce on top and serve at once.

THE ARCHBISHOP CAME TO BREAKFAST

Throughout her life, Rose Kennedy was a devoutly religious Catholic. Most of her life she attended mass daily. In her later years, when it became difficult to get around—remember, she lived to be 104—the Church came to her. Every Sunday, a local priest came to the Compound around ten in the morning to celebrate mass. Occasionally the archbishop of Boston would drop by. This turned Sunday into a major family gathering, especially during the summer months when everyone was in Hyannis Port. From all the Compound houses, relatives came to join the family matriarch for the service. Ethel Kennedy, the Shrivers, and the Smiths were almost always there. Visitors and friends of the family were welcome. Many stayed for brunch, which might turn into lunch, depending upon who wanted to eat what and what their later plans were. Often the kids just grabbed bacon and egg sandwiches and some fruit and cookies to go as they headed out the door of the kitchen to go sailing or play tennis. Most of the adults were content to linger on the porch with a Bloody Mary or Mimosa. If enough people stayed, I'd put out a little breakfast buffet: egg dishes, fruit juices, and an assortment of sweet quick breads. On sunlit days, with the scent of the salty ocean air, the sound of the waves, and the laughter of children in the distance, it was as close to perfect as a Sunday ever comes.

"If enough people stayed, I'd put out a little breakfast buffet…"

After mass on Sundays, brunch was usually a buffet set out in Rose's dining room.

Palm Beach Crab Stack with Poached Eggs

4 SERVINGS

I'D PULL OUT THIS BREAKFAST EXTRAVAGANZA for holidays and special brunches, especially in the spring and summer. Serve with steamed asparagus.

2 English muffins, split in half
4 slices of beefsteak tomato
4 slices of dilled Havarti cheese
½ recipe Hyannis Port Crab Cakes (page 29)
1 tablespoon butter
½ teaspoon distilled white vinegar
4 eggs
1 cup Orange Hollandaise Sauce (recipe on page 116)

1. PREHEAT THE OVEN to 350 degrees F. Toast the English muffins lightly. Arrange the halves in a small baking dish.

2. PLACE 1 SLICE of tomato on each muffin half and top with a slice of the cheese. Set aside.

3. SAUTE THE CRABCAKES in the butter as directed in the recipe on page 29.

4. AT THE SAME TIME, bring a deep skillet of water to a boil with 4 cups water and the vinegar; reduce the heat and keep warm.

5. WHEN THE CRAB CAKES are browned, set one atop each English muffin. Bake the crab stacks for about 5 minutes to melt the cheese.

6. MEANWHILE, ADJUST THE HEAT under your vinegared water so that it is at a simmer. Carefully crack the eggs one at a time and gently slip into the water. Poach for 3 to 4 minutes or to desired doneness; they're best with the whites firm but the yolks still soft.

7. REMOVE THE CRAB STACKS from the oven and place in the center of 4 plates. Top each with a poached egg and cover with ¼ cup of the Orange Hollandaise. Serve at once.

Buttermilk Pancakes

SERVES 3 TO 4

BUTTERMILK, WHICH IS ACTUALLY LOW IN FAT, adds tenderness and a wonderful nutty flavor to anything baked. A big stack of these light pancakes might be cooked up to order or arranged on a platter over a warming candle for a breakfast buffet. The recipe doubles perfectly.

3 eggs
2 tablespoons sugar
Pinch of salt
1½ cups buttermilk
1½ cups cake flour
½ teaspoon baking powder
2 tablespoons butter, melted
¼ cup vegetable oil
Whipped butter and maple syrup, as toppings

1. IN A MEDIUM BOWL, whisk the eggs lightly. Gradually beat in the sugar, salt, and buttermilk until well blended.

2. SIFT THE CAKE FLOUR and baking powder onto the egg mixture and stir in until just blended. Do not beat, or the pancakes will be tough. Blend in the melted butter.

3. HEAT A GRIDDLE or large cast-iron skillet over medium-high heat. Pour half the vegetable oil onto the griddle and spread evenly. When the oil is hot, ladle half the batter onto the griddle to make 4 large pancakes about 5 inches in diameter.

4. COOK UNTIL THE BATTER on the top of the pancakes starts to bubble, 2 to 3 minutes. Flip over and brown the other side, about 2 minutes longer. If the pancakes start browning too fast, reduce the heat slightly. Repeat with the remaining oil and batter. Serve the pancakes at once with whipped butter and maple syrup.

Irish Potato Cakes

SERVES 4 TO 6

BOXITY IS THE GAELIC NAME FOR POTATO PANCAKES. The basic version makes a wonderful accompaniment to any egg dish, like hash browns only better. I often made variations of these with whatever leftovers I had on hand. Sometimes for brunch I'd mix in some bits of Irish smoked salmon and serve them with a poached egg on top and Hollandaise sauce on the side. Or I'd simply top the potato cakes with slices of smoked salmon, a dollop of sour cream, and a sprinkling of chives.

4 large baking potatoes (10 to 12 ounces each)
2 eggs
1 medium onion, finely chopped
3 tablespoons all-purpose flour
Salt and freshly ground pepper
3 tablespoons vegetable oil

1. PEEL THE POTATOES. Shred them on the large holes of a box grater or on the shredding disk of a food processor.

2. IN A LARGE BOWL, whisk the eggs to blend lightly. Whisk in the onion, flour, ½ teaspoon salt, and ¼ teaspoon pepper. Add the shredded potatoes and stir to blend well.

3. HEAT THE OIL in a large heavy skillet over medium-high heat. Spoon the potato mixture into the pan about 3 tablespoons at a time without crowding, in batches if necessary. Flatten with a wide spatula into a pancake about ¼ inch thick. Sauté, turning once, until nicely browned, about 3 minutes per side. Reduce the heat slightly if the outside browns before the potato cakes are cooked through.

Variation

Irish Potato Cakes with Smoked Salmon: Prepare the Irish Potato Cakes as described above, but add 4 ounces smoked salmon, preferably Irish, coarsely chopped, to the eggs along with the shredded potatoes.

spirit—and the infectious good fun. they were honored in a ceremony beneath the Compound flagpole that flew the Stars and Stripes and the Soviet flag in the brisk wind. It was the first time the Soviet flag had flown on our shores. Kara Kennedy gave composer Karen Khatchaturian a bouquet of flowers and a telegram from her aunt Jackie Onassis to give to Maya Plisetskaya, the Bolshoi Ballet star who could not attend the event.

that flew the Stars and Stripes and the Soviet flag in the brisk wind."

Although Mrs. Onassis couldn't be there, she was kind enough to arrange for the performers to take a tour of the President's House before lunch. Composer Khatchaturian bowed before a portrait of President John F. Kennedy and told a reporter from the Boston Herald, "I will never forget this. I am happy to see this place for my own eyes. This one of the strongest feelings I have had in America. This is a sacred place."

The luncheon menu we served the seventy visitors was all-American—and all-Kennedy. It began with clam chowder—made from local quahogs, of course. The main dish was cold roast tenderloin of beef, served with asparagus and potato salad. A basket was filled with my special focaccia rolls and cranberry bread, since cranberries are so typically New England. After lunch, the crowd adjourned to the lawn and the beach, where, even in the brisk March weather, they played touch football, engaged in a bit of soccer, flew kites, and even played netless volleyball.

When the artists returned to the dining room, it was to celebrate the twenty-fifth birthday of one of the dancers. I'd had a heads-up, and in her honor, I had made a chocolate cake with buttercream frosting,topped with a white chocolate sculpture of a ballerina about eight inches high. The young woman was thrilled with the cake—and so was everyone else. The singers expressed their gratitude to all of us with an impromptu concert, which moved me deeply. It was a great privilege to help welcome these extraordinary performers, cultural ambassadors from their country to ours, even before the Cold War had ended.

Blueberry-Orange Bread

MAKES ONE 9-INCH LOAF

BLUEBERRIES ARE ASSOCIATED WITH MAINE, but we had plenty of them on Cape Cod. Because they are a mellow fruit, I like pairing them with orange to pump up their flavor a bit. This bread, by the way, is delicious with the Marmalade Butter on page 194.

2 cups cake flour
1½ teaspoons baking powder
1½ teaspoons baking soda
¾ teaspoon salt
1 stick (4 ounces) butter, at room temperature
¾ cup plus 1 tablespoon granulated sugar
3 eggs
2 teaspoons grated orange zest
1 pint blueberries
Orange Icing (recipe follows)

1. PREHEAT THE OVEN to 375 degrees F. Grease a 9 by 5 by 3-inch loaf pan.

2. IN A MEDIUM BOWL, combine the cake flour, baking powder, baking soda, and salt. Set these dry ingredients aside.

3. USING AN ELECTRIC MIXER, in a large bowl, blend together the butter and ¾ cup of the sugar until light and fluffy. Beat in the eggs and orange zest until well blended. Add the dry ingredients and beat just until mixed. Stir in the blueberries.

4. TURN THE BATTER into the greased pan. Sprinkle the remaining 1 tablespoon sugar on top of the batter.

5. BAKE THE LOAF for 50 minutes, or until a cake tester or wooden toothpick inserted in the center comes out clean. Remove from the oven and let cool slightly. Turn out the loaf and turn right side up. Drizzle the orange icing over the top of the bread. Let cool completely before slicing.

Variation

Cranberry Bread: Make the Blueberry-Orange Bread as described above, but increase the sugar to a 1¼ cups plus 1 tablespoon and substitute 1½ cups of fresh or frozen cranberries for the blueberries.

Orange Icing

MAKES ABOUT ½ CUP

SE FOR A LIGHT GLAZE on top of Blueberry Orange Bread or Cranberry Bread.

1 cup confectioners' sugar
2 tablespoons orange juice
1 egg white
¼ teaspoon vanilla extract

COMBINE all the ingredients in a medium bowl. Whisk until blended and smooth.

At the Compound, everyone was always in motion, sailing, swimming, running, tennis, touch football. When John Jr. went sailing, he rarely set out without a supply of my Chocolate Chip Cookies (page 219) and Brownies (page 220).

Focaccia Rolls with Rosemary, Garlic, and Olives

MAKES 6 ROLLS

RADITIONALLY, FOCACCIA IS MADE INTO one large, flat loaf, but I prefer forming the dough into rolls. Even though they are low, they can be split and used for sandwiches. The rolls go well with almost any salad and make a fine nibble if cut into squares. I always included some of these hot rolls in my bread basket for buffets—morning, noon, and night.

½ package (¼ ounce) active dry yeast, about 1½ teaspoons
¾ cup lukewarm water (100 to 110 degrees F)
1 teaspoon sugar
4 tablespoons extra virgin olive oil
½ cup chopped pitted Kalamata olives
2½ cups bread flour
1 tablespoon coarse salt
1 tablespoon chopped garlic
2 teaspoons chopped fresh rosemary leaves
Freshly ground pepper

1. IN A LARGE MIXING BOWL, combine the yeast, warm water, sugar, and 2 tablespoons of the olive oil. Let stand in a warm place for 5 minutes.

2. ADD THE OLIVES, flour, and 1½ teaspoons of the salt to the yeast. Mix with the dough hook on a standing mixer or knead by hand, just until the flour is incorporated. Cover and let rise for 1 hour.

3. PREHEAT THE OVEN to 450 degrees F. Punch the dough down and divide into 6 equal portions. Form each piece into a fairly flat round, about ½ inch thick, tucking the edges under.

4. ARRANGE THE DOUGH on an oiled baking sheet, leaving at least 2 inches in between rolls. Either prick the tops with a fork or poke with your finger to create dimples all over.

5. BRUSH THE ROLLS generously with the remaining olive oil. Sprinkle the garlic, rosemary, and remaining salt on top. Season with a generous grinding of pepper. Let rise until doubled in volume, about 20 minutes.

6. BAKE THE FOCACCIA for 15 minutes, until golden brown on top and cooked through.

"Your family may or may not have as many kids and visitors as the Kennedy family, but it's my guess that no one can have too many perfect chocolate chip cookies."

Desserts and Beverages

Tents set up on the compound for Kara Kennedy's wedding.

Apple Pie

MAKES A 10-INCH DOUBLE-CRUSTED PIE

TWO THINGS MAKE FOR A GREAT APPLE PIE: a sky-high mound of fresh flavorful apples and plenty of sweet spices. Mine has both, and it bakes up into a beautiful golden dome. To give your crust a professional finish, just before putting it in the oven, brush the pastry with a glaze made from 1 egg beaten with 1 tablespoon milk and dust lightly with sugar.

Pie Crust Dough (recipe follows)
8 Granny Smith apples, peeled, cored, and sliced
1 tablespoon fresh lemon juice
1 cup sugar
Pinch of salt
1 heaping tablespoon cinnamon
½ teaspoon freshly grated nutmeg
¼ teaspoon allspice
2 tablespoons all-purpose flour
1 tablespoon butter, at room temperature

1. PREPARE the Pie Crust Dough and let chill for at least 2 hours as directed.

2. PREHEAT THE OVEN to 350 degrees F. In a large bowl, toss the apple slices with the lemon juice, sugar, salt, cinnamon, nutmeg, allspice, flour, and softened butter.

3. ROLL OUT one of the rounds of dough on a floured board with a floured rolling pin until it's about ⅛ inch thick and 13 to 14 inches in diameter. Roll the dough loosely onto the rolling pin and drape over a 10-inch pie pan. Ease the pastry into the pan without stretching, letting the excess hang over the rim. Trim evenly to ½ inch from the edge.

4. STIR UP THE APPLES and turn them into the pie shell. They should fill it with a high mound.

5. ROLL OUT the second piece of dough in the same way as before to form a round about 12 inches in diameter. Moisten the edge of the bottom crust with water, set the top crust in place, press gently together to seal, and fold the excess dough under all around. Using the tines of a dinner fork, press down on the edge of pie all the way around the pie to seal the dough.

6. WITH THE TIP of a small knife, cut some slits in the pie all around. These are both decorative and allow the steam to vent during the cooking process so the crust is not soggy.

7. BAKE FOR 1 HOUR, or until the apple juices are bubbling and the crust is lightly colored and crisp.

Chef's Note: If you are at all frightened of pie dough, keep the dough well floured and roll it out between two sheets of waxed paper. You will have no trouble at all.

Pie Crust Dough

MAKES ENOUGH FOR A 9- OR 10-INCH DOUBLE-CRUST PIE

2¼ cups all-purpose flour
¾ teaspoon salt
1 stick (4 ounces) butter, at room temperature
½ cup solid white vegetable shortening, such as Crisco
½ cup cold milk

1. IN A MIXING BOWL, toss together the flour and salt. Cut the butter into small cubes and add to the flour. Add the shortening and pinch the flour and fat between your fingertips until the dough is the consistency of very coarse meal; some pea-sized bits of butter are fine.

2. GRADUALLY POUR in the milk while tossing with a fork. Stir until the dough is moistened evenly. Gather the dough together, pressing gently.

3. DIVIDE THE DOUGH in half. Form into 2 balls, then flatten into disks. Dust lightly with flour, wrap the pastry well, and refrigerate for at least 2 hours.

Senator Kennedy in front of the main house with his wife Victoria and Senator John Kerry and wife Teresa Heinz Kerry.

Key Lime Pie

MAKES A 10-INCH PIE; SERVES 8

ROSE KENNEDY SPENT A LOT OF TIME in Palm Beach, and Key lime pie is Florida's official state pie, so she particularly enjoyed this summertime dessert. When fresh key limes are hard to come by, bottled or frozen juice makes a perfectly fine substitute. Some recipes for this dessert call for meringue; I prefer whipped cream.

Graham Cracker and Pistachio Pie Shell (recipe follows)
2 cups milk
½ cup plus 2 tablespoons sugar
3 egg yolks
1½ tablespoons cornstarch
1 tablespoon all-purpose flour
½ cup Key lime juice, fresh or bottled
2 cups heavy cream

1. PREPARE the Graham Cracker and Pistachio Pie Shell as directed and let cool completely.

2. IN A HEAVY MEDIUM SAUCEPAN, preferably enameled cast iron, combine the milk with ¼ cup of the sugar. Bring to a simmer, stirring to dissolve the sugar. Reduce the heat to low.

3. IN A MEDIUM BOWL, whisk together the egg yolks, ¼ cup of the sugar, the cornstarch, flour, and Key lime juice. Gradually pour this mixture into the simmering milk, whisking constantly. Bring to a low boil, whisking until the filling starts to thicken. Immediately remove from the heat.

4. POUR the Key lime filling into the pie shell. Refrigerate until cooled and set, at least 3 hours.

5. IN A CHILLED BOWL with chilled beaters, beat the cream with the remaining 2 tablespoons sugar until stiff peaks form. Using a spatula, spread the whipped cream over the Key lime pie to cover the filling or pipe decoratively on top. Refrigerate until ready to serve.

Graham Cracker and Pistachio Pie Shell

MAKES A 10-INCH PIE SHELL

1½ cups graham cracker crumbs (about 6 ounces)
½ cup finely chopped pistachios
½ cup melted butter

1. PREHEAT THE OVEN to 350 degrees F. In a medium bowl, toss together the graham cracker crumbs and chopped pistachios. Add the melted butter and mix with a fork to moisten evenly.

2. TURN THE CRUMB MIXTURE into a 10-inch pie pan and spread out evenly with your fingers to cover the bottom and sides. Using a second pie pan, press it down firmly on the crumbs to mold them into place, forming the shape of the pie pan.

3. BAKE for 6 to 7 minutes, or until golden brown. Let cool completely before filling.

Banana Cream Pie

MAKES A 10-INCH PIE

EVERYONE LOVES BANANA CREAM PIE—the ultimate comfort dessert. Mine is easy in that there's no fancy arranging. The bananas are stirred right into the custard. Just be sure to allow enough time for chilling the pies.

½ recipe Pie Crust Dough (page 207)
2¼ cups milk
½ cup plus 2 tablespoons sugar
2 egg yolks
½ cup cornstarch
1 tablespoon all-purpose flour
1½ teaspoons butter
1 teaspoon vanilla extract
1 tablespoon banana liqueur
3 bananas, peeled and sliced

1. PREHEAT THE OVEN to 375 degrees F. Prepare the pie dough as directed. Cut out a round of waxed paper or parchment 12 to 13 inches in diameter and set aside.

2. ON A GENEROUSLY floured board, roll out the pie dough about ⅛ inch thick and at least 2 inches larger than the pie pan. Roll the dough up on the rolling pin and place over the pie pan. Ease the pastry into the pan without stretching. Trim the excess dough to ½ inch, fold the edges under, and flute decoratively with your thumb and two fingers.

3. PLACE THE PARCHMENT paper over the dough and fill with about a cup of dried beans to weigh down the dough. Bake for 10 to 12 minutes, or until the dough sets but does not brown. Remove from the oven but leave the oven on. Carefully lift out the paper and beans.

4. RETURN THE PIE SHELL to the oven and bake until crisp and lightly colored, about 15 minutes. Transfer to a wire rack and let cool completely.

5. TO MAKE THE CUSTARD, combine 2 cups of the milk and ¼ cup of the sugar in a nonreactive medium saucepan. Bring to a boil, stirring to dissolve the sugar. Reduce the heat to low.

6. IN A SEPARATE BOWL, whisk together the egg yolks, ¼ cup of the sugar, the cornstarch, flour, and remaining ¼ cup milk until well blended. Whisking constantly, gradually add the egg yolk mixture to the hot milk. Cook, whisking, until the custard starts to thicken. Simmer, whisking, for 2 to 3 minutes. Remove from the heat.

7. WHISK IN THE BUTTER, vanilla, and banana liqueur. Gently stir in the banana slices. Pour into the pie shell and refrigerate until the banana cream filling sets, about 2 hours.

8. WHIP THE HEAVY CREAM with the remaining 2 tablespoons sugar until stiff peaks form. Spread the whipped cream over the banana cream filling. Refrigerate until ready to serve.

Pumpkin Pie

MAKES A 10-INCH PIE

EVERY HALLOWEEN, THE SENATOR and his children would host a pumpkin-carving contest at the Compound. When it was all over, we would end up with plenty of pumpkins, which I would use to make pumpkin puree. I turned it into soups, ravioli, and pies like this one. It was one of my Thanksgiving regulars.

½ recipe Pie Crust Dough (page 207)
2 tablespoons all-purpose flour
3 eggs
2 cups pumpkin puree or canned pumpkin
½ cup packed brown sugar
½ cup granulated sugar
1 teaspoon ground cinnamon
½ teaspoon ground ginger
½ teaspoon salt
Pinch of ground cloves
2 cups light cream or half-and-half
1 cup heavy cream
2 teaspoons confectioners' sugar

1. PREHEAT THE OVEN to 375 degrees F. Prepare the pie dough as directed. Cut out a piece of waxed paper or parchment 12 to 13 inches in diameter.

2. ON A GENEROUSLY floured board, roll out the pie dough about ⅛ inch thick and at least 2 inches larger than the pie pan. Roll the dough up on the rolling pin and place over the pie pan. Ease the pastry into the pan without stretching. Trim the excess dough to ½ inch, fold the edges under, and flute decoratively with your thumb and two fingers.

3. PLACE THE PARCHMENT paper over the dough and fill with about a cup of dried beans to weigh down the dough. Bake for 10 to 12 minutes, or until the dough sets but does not brown. Remove from the oven but leave the oven on. Carefully lift out the paper and beans.

4. IN A MIXING BOWL, whisk together the eggs, pumpkin puree or canned pumpkin, brown sugar, granulated sugar, cinnamon, ginger, salt, cloves, and light cream. Blend well. Pour the filling into the pie shell.

5. BAKE THE PUMPKIN PIE for 45 minutes, or until the filling is firm. Remove to a wire rack and let cool completely.

6. WHIP THE HEAVY CREAM with the confectioners' sugar until stiff peaks form. Serve each slice of pie with a dollop of whipped cream on top.

KARA KENNEDY'S JOYOUS WEDDING

Senator Ted Kennedy had stood in for his brothers John and Bobby when he walked Caroline and two of Bobby's daughters down the aisle at their weddings. But those emotional journeys did not fully prepare him for his only daughter Kara's wedding in September 1990. "The easiest job was walking Kara down the aisle," the Senator said that day. "The hardest job was giving her away."

The job I was asked to do for Kara's wedding was not nearly as difficult, but it was a tremendous honor: she had asked me to make her wedding cake. Soon after, when she invited my wife and me to attend the wedding, I was even more moved. When the day came, the church was full of joyous Kennedys—and full of music, the highlight of which was a gospel choir rendition of "Oh, Happy Day." Kara herself remarked that the song "nearly lifted the roof off the church."

The buffet dinner took place in a huge tent on the lawn of the compound. When it came time to cut the cake, the room became very quiet. Kara asked me to come up, essentially to take a bow and stand near my ornate creation. It was a six-tiered chocolate cake with fruit filling, topped with pulled

"When it came time to cut the cake…Kara asked me to come up,

sugarflowers—one of my specialties—and a carved chocolate replica of her Uncle John's beloved boat, the *Victura*, about to set sail on the bottom tier.

As I threaded my way across the floor, around dozens of tables filled with family and celebrated guests, everyone began chanting my name. Hundreds of voices suddenly rang out with, "Neil! Neil! Neil! Neil!"

The celebratory chanting was a family tradition. At Rose Kennedy's 100th birthday, just months before, the sounds of folks chanting, "Grandma! Grandma! Grandma" as we presented the cake to her, were overwhelming. But this kind of public attention had never before been bestowed on me. It was a great moment for me, personally and professionally.

And I'm proud to say that the cake disappeared almost as fast as the chocolate chip cookies and brownies always did.

essentially to take a bow and stand near my ornate creation."

FACING PAGE: *Senator Ted Kennedy and his daughter Kara, as he prepares to give her away.*
TOP: *Jacqueline Kennedy Onassis and son John emerging from Kara Kennedy's wedding to Michael Allen.*
ABOVE LEFT: *For Kara's cake, Neil outdid himself with his pulled sugar artistry.*
The boat is a replica of Kara's beloved uncle President John Fitzgerald Kennedy's Victura.
ABOVE RIGHT: *Neil putting the finishing touches on Kara's six-tiered cake.*

Kara's Chocolate Cake

MAKES A 10-INCH LAYER CAKE; SERVES 16

This is the recipe I used to make the elaborate cake for Kara Kennedy's wedding to Michael Allen. Covered with a Grand Marnier buttercream and filled with fresh berries and cream, the cake was decorated with bouquets of pulled sugar flowers I made along with a white chocolate replica of their uncle President John F. Kennedy's boat, the Victura, which Kara and Michael loved to sail on.

One-Bowl Chocolate Butter Cake (recipe follows)

3 tablespoons Chambord raspberry liqueur

1 cup heavy cream

1 teaspoon confectioners' sugar

1½ cups fresh berries: raspberries, sliced strawberries and/or blackberries

Grand Marnier Buttercream Frosting (page 216)

1. BAKE THE ONE-BOWL CHOCOLATE BUTTER cake as directed below. It will be easier to work with if you bake it a day or two in advance.

2. TO FILL THE CAKE, use a long serrated knife to carefully split the cake in half horizontally to make 2 layers. Sprinkle 2 tablespoons of the Chambord over the cut side of the rounded half; this will be your bottom layer.

3. IN A CHILLED BOWL with cold beaters, whip the cream with the confectioners' sugar and remaining 1 tablespoon Chambord until stiff. Spread over the cake. Arrange the berries on top of the whipped cream, distributing them evenly and reserving a few for garnish. Set the other half of the cake in place, bottom side up.

4. COVER THE TOP and sides of the cake with the Grand Marnier buttercream. There will be enough so that you can pipe some decoratively, if you like. Garnish with the reserved berries.

One-Bowl Chocolate Butter Cake

MAKES ONE 10-INCH LAYER

2 sticks (8 ounces) butter, at room temperature
2 cups sugar
1 tablespoon vanilla extract
4 ounces unsweetened chocolate, melted
5 eggs
2 cups sifted cake flour
1 teaspoon baking soda
1 teaspoon salt
1 cup milk

1. PREHEAT THE OVEN to 350 degrees F. Grease the bottom and sides of a 10-inch cake pan. Line the bottom with a round of parchment or waxed paper and grease the paper.

2. WITH AN ELECTRIC MIXER, beat together the butter, sugar, vanilla, and melted chocolate. Add the eggs one at a time, beating well after each addition. Gradually beat in the flour. Then add the baking soda and salt. Gradually beat in the milk. Turn the batter into the prepared cake pan.

3. BAKE FOR 25 TO 30 MINUTES, or until a pick inserted in the center comes out clean and the cake is just beginning to pull away from the sides of the pan. Transfer to a wire rack and let cool. Gently remove the cake from the pan, wrap in plastic, and refrigerate until ready to decorate.

Senator Kennedy on the water with son Teddy Jr., daughter Kara, and Ted Jr.'s wife, Kiki.

Grand Marnier Buttercream Frosting

MAKES ABOUT 3 CUPS

PROFESSIONALS OFTEN USE A MIX of half butter and half shortening, as I do here. It results in a lighter buttercream that is more stable. However, you may use all butter, if you prefer.

2½ sticks (10 ounces) butter, at room temperature
1¼ cups solid white vegetable shortening
1 box (16 ounces) confectioners' sugar
Pinch of salt
¼ cup Grand Marnier
6 egg whites, preferably organic
2 tablespoons fresh lemon juice
1 tablespoon vanilla extract

1. WITH AN ELECTRIC MIXER set on low, cream together the butter, shortening, confectioners' sugar, and salt. Blend well, stopping from time to time to scrape down the sides with a spatula.

2. ADD THE GRAND MARNIER, egg whites, and lemon juice. Beat on high speed until the buttercream comes together and is light and fluffy.

3. IF NOT USING right away, cover and refrigerate. Remove from the refrigerator 1 or 2 hours before use so that the buttercream softens enough to spread easily.

Irish Bread Pudding

SERVES 6

UNLIKE MANY BREAD PUDDINGS, which are leaden, this one is a lush baked custard, flavored with a serious amount of Irish Cream and thickened with a modest amount of bread crumbs. For a dinner party, individual portions are nice; a single dish may be easier to prepare for family dinners.

8 eggs
1 cup milk
½ cup sugar
½ cup Bailey's Irish Cream
1 teaspoon vanilla extract
Pinch of freshly grated nutmeg
2 cups fresh bread crumbs
1 tablespoon butter, slightly softened
Whipped cream or vanilla ice cream, as accompaniment

1. PREHEAT THE OVEN to 325 degrees F. Set a roasting pan on the middle rack of the oven and fill it with about 1 inch of hot water.

2. IN A LARGE BOWL, beat the eggs and milk together. Whisk in the sugar, Bailey's Irish Cream, vanilla, and nutmeg. Mix in the bread crumbs.

3. USE THE BUTTER to grease six 8-ounce soufflé dishes or a shallow 3-quart casserole. Pour in the breaded custard.

4. BAKE THE BREAD PUDDING for 20 minutes, or until set. Transfer to a wire rack and let cool for about 15 minutes. Run a small knife around the edges of the soufflé dishes to release the puddings. Cut the large pudding into squares.

5. SERVE THE BREAD PUDDING warm on dessert plates with a spoonful of whipped cream or a scoop of vanilla ice cream.

Big-Batch Chocolate Chip Cookies

MAKES 3 DOZEN 4-INCH COOKIES

YOUR FAMILY MAY OR MAY NOT HAVE as many kids and visitors as the Kennedy family, but it's my guess that no one can have too many of these perfect chocolate chip cookies. If you like nuts in yours, add 1 cup chopped macadamia nuts to the dough along with the chocolate chips.

1½ pounds butter
1¾ cups packed light brown sugar
1½ cups granulated sugar
5 eggs
1 tablespoon vanilla extract
4½ cups all-purpose flour
1½ teaspoons baking soda
1 teaspoon salt
3 cups chocolate chips

1. USING AN ELECTRIC MIXER on medium speed, beat the butter with the brown sugar and granulated sugar until light and fluffy. Beat in the eggs and vanilla. Add the flour, baking soda, salt, and 2 tablespoons water. Blend well. Stir in the chocolate chips by hand until evenly distributed. Refrigerate the dough until you're ready to bake.

2. PREHEAT THE OVEN to 350 degrees F. Lightly grease 2 cookie sheets. You'll need to bake the cookies in batches.

3. USING TWO SPOONS, scoop up about a tablespoon of dough with one and push it off onto the cookie sheet with the other. Make sure you space out the cookies, because they will spread out when cooking. Leave at least 2 inches in between.

4. BAKE THE COOKIES for about 10 minutes, or until golden brown. (Depending upon your oven, you may want to rotate the sheets after 5 minutes.) Transfer to wire racks and let cool.

Chef's Note: As with most cookies, you can make these by hand, but because of the volume of the ingredients, I recommend an electric mixer.

Brownies

MAKES 12 LARGE BROWNIES

PURE CHOCOLATE—NO FRUIT OR NUTS—is what distinguishes my brownies, and it was this recipe along with the chocolate chip cookies on page 219 that I always kept stocked for the kids. John Jr., in particular, loved them, and with all the summer sports—sailing, swimming, running, touch football—he and his friends could go through mountains of them. They were such a family favorite, Caroline and Jackie requested them for the dessert table at the wedding week luncheon they threw for Maria Shriver.

1 stick (4 ounces) butter
2 ounces unsweetened chocolate
2 eggs
1 cup sugar
½ cup all-purpose flour
1 teaspoon vanilla extract

1. PREHEAT THE OVEN to 325 degrees F. Butter an 8-inch square baking pan.

2. IN A SMALL SAUCEPAN, melt the butter and chocolate over low heat, stirring and taking care not to scorch the chocolate. Whisk to blend well.

3. IN A MEDIUM BOWL, beat the eggs and sugar together until the mixture is lightened and forms a slowly dissolving ribbon when the beaters are lifted, about 2 minutes. Beat in the melted chocolate and butter. Add the flour and vanilla and mix just until blended. Turn the batter into the prepared pan.

4. BAKE FOR 25 MINUTES, or until just done. Do not overbake, or the brownies will be dry. A cake tester or wooden pick inserted in the center should come out with a few crumbs still sticking to it. Remove to a wire rack and let cool, then cut the brownies into 12 squares.

Wexford Trifle

SERVES 8 TO 12

Summer is berry season on the Cape, and this dessert shows off the beautiful fruit at its colorful best. It's a great warm-weather recipe for entertaining. For this recipe, if your cake is a day or so old, it will only improve the dessert, because slightly stale cake soaks up more of the fruit juices and syrup.

5 cups mixed berries: blueberries, raspberries, blackberries, sliced strawberries
1 cup Raspberry Chardonnay Sauce (page 231)
¼ cup granulated sugar
2 tablespoons Irish Mist liqueur
1 pound sponge cake, cut into 1-inch squares
4 cups Irish Mist Pastry Cream (recipe follows)
2 cups heavy cream
2 tablespoons confectioners' sugar
Fresh currants (optional)

1. PUT ALL THE BERRIES in a mixing bowl, add the Raspberry Chardonnary Sauce and toss gently, being careful not to crush the berries. Let stand while you prepare the rest of the dessert.

2. IN A SMALL SAUCEPAN, combine the sugar with ½ cup water. Bring to a boil, stirring to dissolve the sugar. Remove the syrup from the heat and let cool; then add the Irish Mist.

3. CHOOSE A TRIFLE BOWL, or any large glass bowl, preferably with straight sides. Cover the bottom with pieces of sponge cake. Drizzle a little of the syrup over the cake to moisten lightly. Cover with a layer of pastry cream and then one of berries, making sure to include the raspberry sauce and any juices that collect. Repeat these layers until you've filled the bowl at least three quarters of the way up and used up all the cake, mixed berries, and pastry cream.

4. IN A CHILLED BOWL with cold beaters, whip the cream with the confectioners' sugar until stiff. Either use a pastry bag with a star tip to decorate the top of the trifle with rosettes of whipped cream or simply dollop the cream on top and swirl it decoratively. Garnish with some sprigs of fresh currants, if you have them.

Chef's Note: Make the pastry cream at least an hour in advance here, so that it has a chance to cool before you begin assembling the trifle.

Irish Mist Pastry Cream

MAKES ABOUT 2½ CUPS

2 cups plus 2 tablespoons milk
¼ cup granulated sugar
2 egg yolks
2 tablespoons cornstarch
1 tablespoon all-purpose flour
1 teaspoon butter
1 teaspoon vanilla extract
2 to 3 tablespoons Irish Mist liqueur

1. BRING 2 CUPS of the milk to a simmer with 2 tablespoons of the sugar. Reduce the heat to low and keep warm.

2. IN A SMALL BOWL, whisk together the egg yolks with the remaining 2 tablespoons sugar, the cornstarch, flour, and remaining 2 tablespoons milk until smooth and well blended. Gradually whisk the hot milk into this mixture. Return to the saucepan and bring to a boil, whisking until the pastry cream thickens. Reduce the heat to low and simmer, whisking, for 2 minutes.

3. IMMEDIATELY REMOVE from the heat and scrape into a bowl. Whisk in the Irish Mist. Let cool slightly, then cover with a sheet of plastic wrap pressed right onto the surface of the custard to prevent a skin from forming. Refrigerate until chilled. If the custard has thickened too much when you go to use it, simply whisk briefly to lighten it.

Banana Soufflé

SERVES 4

SOUFFLÉS ARE ONE OF MY SPECIALTIES. I don't think there's a nicer—or more dramatic—dessert you can offer at a dinner party. And notice, my technique is easy: no paper collars required. Individual portions are the nicest way to go. It's worth the small investment in these dishes. But if you don't have them, make one large soufflé in a 1½-quart soufflé dish and increase the baking time by 5 to 7 minutes.

3 tablespoons butter
⅓ cup all-purpose flour
¾ cup granulated sugar, plus more for coating the dishes
¼ teaspoon salt
1 cup milk
½ ripe banana, mashed
5 large eggs, separated
¼ cup banana liqueur
1 tablespoon vanilla extract
⅛ teaspoon cream of tartar
Banana Rum Sauce (recipe follows) and whipped cream

1. PREHEAT THE OVEN to 400 degrees F. Use about 1 tablespoon of the butter to grease the insides of four 8-ounce soufflé dishes. Dust the bottom and sides of each dish with a little sugar to coat evenly.

2. IN A SMALL SAUCEPAN, combine the flour, ¼ cup of the sugar, and the salt. Gradually whisk in the milk, set over medium-high heat, and bring to a boil, whisking constantly until the mixture thickens to a paste and sticks to the side of the pot, 3 to 4 minutes. Make sure you beat well enough to remove any lumps.

3. SCRAPE THIS PASTE into a mixing bowl. Add the remaining 2 tablespoons butter, the mashed banana, egg yolks, banana liqueur, and vanilla. Whisk until well blended.

4. IN A LARGE MIXING BOWL, whip the egg whites with the remaining ½ cup sugar and the cream of tartar until soft peaks form.

5. FOLD ABOUT ONE THIRD of the egg whites into the soufflé base to lighten the mixture. Then fold in the remaining egg whites just until no white streaks remain. Divide among the soufflé dishes; it should reach almost up to the top of each dish. Run your index finger around the inside rim of each dish to create a little groove around the soufflé mixture. This allows the soufflé to rise straight up without overflowing.

6. BAKE ON THE MIDDLE SHELF of the oven for 20 minutes. Serve immediately with Banana Rum Sauce and whipped cream, if you like.

Banana Rum Sauce

SERVES 4

2 ripe bananas, peeled and sliced
5 tablespoons butter
½ cup packed brown sugar
2 tablespoons Myers's Rum

1. IN A LARGE HEAVY SKILLET, melt the butter over medium-high heat. Add the bananas and sauté, turning, until very lightly browned, 2 to 3 minutes.

2. SPRINKLE ON THE brown sugar, reduce the heat to medium-low, and stir gently until the sugar melts and form a sauce around the banana slices, about 3 minutes. Add the rum and remove from the heat. Serve warm.

An example of Neil's chocolate and pulled sugar artistry.

Crème Brûlée

SERVES 4

OLDER RECIPES FOR CRÈME BRÛLÉE call for chilling them and then running them under a hot broiler to get the crackly caramel crust, which is the hallmark of a great crème brûlée. If you've ever tried this, you know it is imperfect. The only way to get the crust you want is to melt the brown sugar with a propane torch. Home kitchen models are available in kitchenware catalogs and cookware shops, but I recommend a small, inexpensive plumber's torch from a hardware store. Just be careful with the open flame.

8 egg yolks
¾ cup granulated sugar
2½ cups light cream or half-and-half
1 teaspoon vanilla extract
4 teaspoons light brown sugar

1. PREHEAT THE OVEN to 350 degrees F. Set a shallow roasting pan half-filled with hot water on the middle shelf of the oven.

2. IN A MIXING BOWL, whisk the egg yolks lightly. Gradually whisk in the granulated sugar and then the light cream and vanilla. Ladle this custard into four 8-ounce ramekins or soufflé dishes and carefully set in the water bath in the oven.

3. COOK THE CUSTARDS for 40 minutes, or until firm. Carefully remove from the water bath, being careful not to get them wet. Sprinkle 1 teaspoon of brown sugar over the top of each and melt with a small blowtorch. Serve the crème brûlée at once or refrigerate for up to 4 hours.

Variation

Berried Crème Brûlée: Toss 1 cup of blackberries, raspberries, and/or blueberries with 3 tablespoons sugar. After glazing the custards as described above, top each dessert with about ¼ cup of the sugared berries, allowing them to spill over onto the plate. Garnish with a sprig of fresh mint and a dollop of whipped cream.

THE SPIRIT OF ROSE (1890–1995)

She meant it when she said, "Life isn't a matter of milestones, but of moments." Rose Fitzgerald Kennedy had amassed 104 years of extraordinary moments—and a few milestones, too—by the time she passed away in 1995. By any measure, she was a remarkable woman who left a remarkable legacy.

On her 100th birthday, a few short blocks from her house on the Compound, a grassy street corner was turned into a small garden to honor her. A plaque on a large rock sits in the center, surrounded by rose bushes. The message on the plaque offers a fitting introduction:

"Rose Fitzgerald Kennedy had amassed 104 years

Rose Fitzgerald Kennedy at 100
A woman of valor whose
effervescent spirit,
compassion, and vision helped
shape American history

Rose Fitzgerald Kennedy is best known for being mother to nine children, including three U.S. Senators (Jack, Robert, and Edward), one of whom became President. Three of her sons died tragically in the service of their country, Joseph Jr., in a military plane crash during World War II, Jack and Robert, both assassinated by gunmen. Rose was the daughter of the first mayor of Boston, whose own parents had been immigrants, and mother to the country's first—and last—Irish Catholic president. She had a privileged upbringing that included study at the New England Conservatory, the Convent of the Sacred Heart in Boston, and a Catholic finishing school in the Netherlands.

Although she came of age at a time when women of her class were meant only to be mothers, wives, and decorative society figures, Rose had other inclinations. Her faith, education, and political background inspired her to teach catechism to Boston's poor and to organize groups to discuss politics and news. In 1914, she married an ambitious, hard-driving young bank president and Harvard graduate, Joseph P. Kennedy. He would become a millionaire many times over and ambassador to England in the years leading up to World War II.

Rose instilled her religious and intellectual values in her children. The dinner table was an educational institution where every night the youngsters had to prepare by first reading news articles their mother had pinned to a nearby bulletin board. Over the meal, they had to discuss and debate them. Silence was not an option; neither was timidity or indecision. Rose played "Twenty Questions" with them, taught them to read maps and read poetry. One story goes that when Ethel married Bobby Kennedy, she began studying encyclopedias and almanacs, learning everything she could to fit in with the family.

Rose Kennedy suffered more tragedies than any one person ought to be allowed. She outlived four of her children and two of her twenty-eight grandchildren. But she was sustained by her lifelong work for the mentally retarded, in honor of her daughter Rosemary, by her faith, and by the love of the family she and her husband had created.

She took everything seriously, including her name. The living room curtains and the upholstery had a rose design, her Aynsley china was adorned with small roses, and the rug under the dining room table had a box design, and inside each box was a rose. Keeping with that theme, for every special occasion, I decorated cakes and desserts with pink and red roses made of pulled sugar, one of my specialties, and a gift I was always eager to bestow on this wonderful woman.

of extraordinary moments—and a few milestones…"

FACING PAGE: *Rose remembered with love by the city of Hyannis Port.*
TOP: *Rose's birthday cake for the family's private party with their beloved mother, grandmother, and matriarch.*
ABOVE: *Neil helping to carry the portrait of Rose Kennedy as a young girl out to one of the big pink and white–striped tents set up for the formal celebration of her 100th birthday.*

Rose Kennedy's Chocolate Soufflé

SERVES 4 OR 6

Rose Kennedy loved chocolate, and soufflés were one of the family's favorite dinner-party desserts. After attending a dedication of the Rose Garden in Hyannis Port for Rose Kennedy, there was a large family celebratory dinner. I served a chocolate soufflé, which I garnished with a beautiful bright pink pulled sugar rose. It was big hit.

You can offer an equally beautiful presentation by adorning the dessert plates with candied rose petals or even a fresh rosebud.

3 tablespoons butter, softened
1 cup plus 1 tablespoon sugar
⅓ cup all-purpose flour
¼ cup unsweetened cocoa powder
Pinch of salt
1 cup whole milk
6 large eggs, separated
3 ounces semisweet chocolate, melted
¼ cup Cognac or brandy
⅛ teaspoon cream of tartar
Sweetened whipped cream
Raspberry Chardonnay Sauce (recipe follows)

1. PREHEAT THE OVEN to 400 degrees F. Use 1 tablespoon of the butter to grease four 8-ounce straight-sided ramekins, six 6-ounce ramekins, or a 1½-quart soufflé dish. Dust the bottom and sides with 1 tablespoon of the sugar.

2. IN A HEAVY MEDIUM SAUCEPAN, combine ½ cup of the sugar with the flour, cocoa powder, and salt. Whisk in the milk to blend well. Set over medium-high heat and cook, whisking constantly, until the mixture boils, thickens to a paste, and begins to stick to the side of the pot, 3 to 4 minutes.

3. IMMEDIATELY REMOVE from the heat and scrape the chocolate paste into a heatproof mixing bowl. Whisk in the remaining 2 tablespoons butter, then the egg yolks, the melted chocolate, and the Cognac or brandy.

4. IN A CLEAN BOWL with clean beaters, whip the egg whites with the cream of tartar until frothy. Gradually add the remaining ½ cup sugar and beat until soft peaks form.

5. FOLD ABOUT A THIRD of the whipped egg whites into the chocolate soufflé base to lighten it. Then gently fold in the remaining egg whites just until no white streaks remain. Divide among the ramekins or turn into the soufflé dish; it should reach almost up to the top of each dish. Run your index finger around the inside rim of each dish to create a little groove around the soufflé mixture. This allows the soufflé to rise straight up without overflowing.

6. BAKE FOR 20 MINUTES, or 15 minutes if you are using a convection oven; if using the large soufflé dish, bake about 10 minutes longer. The soufflé(s) should be puffed and browned on top but still soft in the center. Serve immediately, with Raspberry Chardonnay Sauce and whipped cream in separate sauceboats on the side, so everyone can help themselves.

Raspberry Chardonnay Sauce

MAKES ABOUT 1½ CUPS

1 pint fresh raspberries

½ cup sugar

½ cup Chardonnay or other white wine

1. PUREE THE RASPBERRIES. Pass the puree through a sieve to remove the seeds.

2. IN A SMALL NONREACTIVE SAUCEPAN, bring the sugar and wine to a boil, stirring to dissolve the sugar. Reduce the heat and simmer for 5 minutes to evaporate the alcohol.

3. ADD THE FRESH RASPBERRY PUREE and simmer for 5 minutes longer. Remove from the heat and let cool, then refrigerate until ready for use.

Rose Kennedy's Chocolate Soufflé complete with whipped cream, Raspberry Chardonnay Sauce, and Chef Connolly's trademark pulled sugar rose.

Grand Marnier Soufflé

SERVES 4

A GENEROUS AMOUNT OF ORANGE ZEST is the secret to this elegant soufflé. Use a Microplane if you have one for easiest grating. And be sure to take off only the colored outer skin; the white pith underneath is bitter.

3 tablespoons butter
¾ cup plus 1 tablespoon sugar
⅓ cup all-purpose flour
¼ teaspoon salt
1 cup whole milk
1 tablespoon grated orange zest
5 large eggs, separated
¼ cup Grand Marnier
⅛ teaspoon cream of tartar

1. PREHEAT THE OVEN to 400 degrees F. Use 1 tablespoon of the butter to coat the bottom and sides of four 8-ounce soufflé dishes. Dust each with 1 tablespoon of the sugar to coat evenly.

2. IN A SMALL SAUCEPAN, combine the flour, ¼ cup of the sugar, and the salt. Gradually whisk in the milk, set over medium-high heat, and bring to a boil, whisking constantly until the mixture boils, thickens to a paste, and sticks to the side of the pot, 3 to 4 minutes. Make sure you whip any lumps out of the paste.

3. SCRAPE THE HOT PASTE into a bowl. Beat in the remaining 2 tablespoons butter, the orange zest, egg yolks, and Grand Marnier. Blend well.

4. IN A LARGE BOWL, beat the egg whites with the remaining ½ cup sugar and the cream of tarter until soft peaks form. Fold about one third of the egg whites into the soufflé base to lighten the mixture. Then fold in the remaining egg whites just until no white streaks remain. Divide among the soufflé dishes; it should reach almost up to the top of each dish. Run your index finger around the inside rim of each dish to create a little groove around the soufflé mixture. This allows the soufflé to rise straight up without overflowing.

5. BAKE ON THE MIDDLE SHELF of the oven for 20 minutes. Serve immediately, with Grand Marnier Sauce and whipped cream, if you like.

Grand Marnier Sauce

MAKES ABOUT ¾ CUP

1 cup fresh orange juice
¼ cup packed light brown sugar
¼ cup finely shredded orange zest
2 tablespoons Grand Marnier

1. IN A SMALL SAUCEPAN, combine the orange juice, brown sugar, and orange zest. Bring to a boil, stirring to dissolve the brown sugar. Continue to cook over medium-high until the sauce is slightly thickened and syrupy, 4 to 5 minutes.

2. REMOVE FROM THE HEAT and stir in the Grand Marnier. Set aside to cool at room temperature until ready to use.

Photos on the piano in Rose's living room hold images of her husband and of the beloved children she so tragically lost.

Chardonnay Poached Pears with Raspberry Sauce

SERVES 4

DESSERTS ARE MY GREAT LOVE. Chocolate and sugar work are two of my specialties. When I was actively competing in international chef's competitions, I was one of the few to garner a perfect score in the Culinary Olympics. All this is to explain why my dessert presentations usually include a few extra elements, like the sugar cookies and chocolate leaves I often use to decorate these delightful pears.

4 Anjou or Bartlett pears
1 bottle (750 ml) Chardonnay or other full-flavored dry white wine
1½ cups sugar
½ cup Raspberry Chardonnay Sauce (page 231)
4 scoops of vanilla ice cream
Chocolate leaves or fresh mint leaves and whipped cream, for garnish

1. PEEL THE PEARS and remove the cores from the bottom so the fruit looks whole, and the woody stems are intact.

2. IN A LARGE NONREACTIVE SAUCEPAN, combine the white wine and sugar. Bring to a simmer, stirring to dissolve the sugar. Add the whole pears, cover, and reduce the heat to medium-low. Simmer for 15 to 20 minutes, or until the pears are tender.

3. REMOVE FROM THE HEAT and let cool. Then refrigerate the pears in their cooking liquid until they are chilled, at least 2 hours. (The pears can be poached a day in advance.)

4. TO SERVE, place the pears in dessert dishes. Spoon 3 to 4 tablespoons of raspberry sauce over and around each pear. Garnish the pears with chocolate leaves or fresh mint leaves and a spoonful of whipped cream.

Chocolate Leaves

MAKES ABOUT 8

THE BEST CHOCOLATE TO USE HERE is bittersweet or semisweet "couverture," which means it contains roughly one third cocoa butter for a lovely sheen. The gloss is also affected by how the chocolate is "tempered," that is, melted to an exact temperature and then cooled properly. If you want to attach a chocolate leave to a dessert, simply use a little melted chocolate as glue.

6 ounces dark sweetened chocolate, preferably couverture, chopped

Fresh unsprayed citrus, rose, or other nontoxic leaves

1. MELT TWO THIRDS (4 ounces) of the chocolate in a double boiler over hot—not simmering—water. Make sure the top pan is above the water, not touching. Remove from the heat as soon as the chocolate is melted. If you use a thermometer, it should register 120 degrees F.

2. NOW ADD THE remaining chopped chocolate. Remove the top of the double boiler from the heat and continue stirring until the chocolate is cooled to blood temperature.

3. BRUSH THE MELTED CHOCOLATE over the leaves. Set them on a small tray and refrigerate for about 3 to 4 minutes, then peel the leaf off the chocolate.

Hot Mulled Cider

SERVES 18 TO 24

WHEN A DAMP CHILL WOULD ROLL in off the ocean in the fall and winter months, nothing was more warming than a mug of spiced hot cider. I always made it nonalcoholic so the children could enjoy it, too. Besides tasting delicious, the brew made the house smell wonderful and especially during the holidays, invariably drew everyone into my kitchen.

1 gallon apple cider, preferably fresh
4 seedless oranges, scrubbed and cut in half
3 cinnamon sticks
8 whole cloves
½ teaspoon freshly grated nutmeg
2 cups honey

1. POUR THE APPLE CIDER into a large stainless steel or enameled cast-iron pot and set over medium heat. Squeeze the juice from the oranges into the cider. Then toss in the orange halves as well. Add the cinnamon sticks, whole cloves, grated nutmeg, and honey.

2. WHEN BUBBLES APPEAR around the edge of the cider, reduce the heat to low and simmer, uncovered, for about 1 hour to develop the flavors.

3. SERVE RIGHT from the pot or pour into a crock and ladle into mugs.

Bellini

THE ORIGINAL BELLINI WAS REPORTEDLY INVENTED at Harry's Bar in Venice, Italy in 1948 by Giuseppe Cipriani. His original recipe was made by mixing Prosecco, Italian sparkling wine, into pureed fresh white peaches. What's not to like? The combination makes a delightful summer drink, and at the Compound, we devised many variations, using different pureed fruits and the house champagne: Dom Perignon.

Peach Bellini

FOR EACH DRINK:

1 part fresh peach puree
2 parts iced champagne or other sparkling white wine

SPOON THE FRUIT puree into a fluted champagne glass. Pour in the champagne and stir to blend.

Pear Bellini

Prepare drink as for Peach Bellini, but use:

1 part fresh pear puree
2 parts iced champagne or other sparkling white wine

Raspberry Bellini

Prepare drink as for Peach Bellini, but use:

1 part fresh rasberry puree
2 parts iced champagne or other sparkling white wine

Mango Bellini

Prepare drink as for Peach Bellini, but use:

1 part fresh mango puree
2 parts iced champagne or other sparkling white wine

Strawberry Bellini

Prepare drink as for Peach Bellini, but use:

1 part fresh strawberry puree
2 parts iced champagne or other sparkling white wine

Party Pitcher of Bloody Marys

SERVES 12 TO 16

ESPECIALLY FOR BRUNCHES, I'd whip up a batch of these zippy Bloody Marys. Guests got a kick of the way I'd garnish the glass: In addition to the standard celery rib with leaves, I'd attach a big cooked shrimp to the side of each drink.

1 bottle (1 litre) Stolichnaya or your favorite vodka
1 large can (46 ounces) V-8 juice
1 cup prepared white horseradish
2 tablespoons fresh lemon juice
1 tablespoon fresh lime juice
2 tablespoons Thai-style hot sauce, such as Srirachi
2 tablespoons Worcestershire sauce
½ teaspoon Tabasco, or more to taste
1 tablespoon celery salt
1 tablespoon salt
1 tablespoon black pepper

MIX ALL THE INGREDIENTS together in a large pitcher. Pour over ice in tall highball glasses or in large stemmed water glasses.

Martini

THE MARTINI IS ENJOYING A HUGE REVIVAL, but at the summer Compound, they never went out of style. To really enjoy this drink, you have to have the right glasses, or it won't look like a martini. They come in all sizes and prices; so if you're planning to serve this cocktail in quantity, keep an eye out for sales of glasses.

The classic martini is made with 2½ ounces (⅓ cup) gin and ½ ounce (1 tablespoon) dry vermouth, though these days some people prefer them even drier with just a splash of vermouth. The alcohol is poured over ice in a cocktail shaker and either stirred or shaken until it is chilled. Then the drink is strained and served straight up, without ice, in a chilled martini glass. Garnish with a twist of lemon or an olive. There are thousands of variations. Here are some martinis we served at the Compound.

Apple Martini

FOR EACH DRINK:

2 ounces (¼ cup) Stolichnaya or other vodka
1½ ounces (3 tablespoons) Maria Brizzard Manzanita or other apple liqueur
1½ ounces Hiram Walker sour apple liqueur
Splash of sweet and sour mix

POUR ALL the ingredients over ice in a cocktail shaker. Stir, then strain into a martini glass.

Irish Chocolate Martini

FOR EACH DRINK:

Chocolate syrup, preferably Hershey's
2 ounces (¼ cup) Stolichnaya or other vodka
1 ounce (2 tablespoons) Godiva chocolate liqueur
2 ounces (¼ cup) Bailey's Irish Cream

DIP A MARTINI GLASS in chocolate syrup to coat the rim. Pour the vodka, chocolate liqueur, and Irish Cream over ice in a cocktail shaker. Cover and shake until chilled. Strain into the martini glass.

Melon Martini

FOR EACH DRINK:

2 ounces (¼ cup) Stolichnaya or other vodka
1 ounce (2 tablespoons) Midori melon liqueur
Splash of fresh orange juice
Melon balls, for garnish

POUR THE VODKA, melon liqueur, and orange juice over ice in a cocktail shaker. Cover and shake until chilled. Strain into a martini glass and garnish with 2 melon balls on a toothpick.

Hyannis Port Martini

FOR EACH DRINK:

2 ounces (¼ cup) Bombay Sapphire or other gin
1½ ounces (3 tablespoons) Blue Curaçao, such as Hiram Walker's
½ ounce (1 tablespoon) Blueberry Pucker
Splash of cranberry juice

POUR ALL THE INGREDIENTS over ice in a cocktail shaker. Cover and shake until chilled. Strain into a martini glass.

Mimosa

IT'S SAID THE MIMOSA COCKTAIL, named after the yellow flower, was invented at the Ritz Hotel in Paris, France. Wherever it came from, it's become a great American brunch drink and was a favorite at many Kennedy daytime events.

FOR EACH DRINK:

1 part fresh orange juice
2 parts champagne or other sparkling white wine
Fresh strawberry, for garnish

POUR THE ORANGE JUICE and champagne into a champagne flute. Stir gently. Attach a berry to the rim of the glass.

Midori Mimosa

FOR EACH DRINK:

1 ounce (2 tablespoons) Midori melon liqueur
2 teaspoons sweet-and-sour mix
4 ounces (½ cup) champagne or other sparkling white wine
Melon ball, for garnish

POUR THE MIDORI liqueur and sweet-and-sour mix into a fluted champagne glass. Add the sparkling wine and stir gently. Garnish with a melon ball on a toothpick.

Cape Cod Mimosa

FOR EACH DRINK:

1 part cranberry juice
2 Dom Perignon or other champagne or sparkling white wine

POUR THE CRANBERRY juice into a fluted champagne glass. Then fill the glass with the sparkling wine.

Irish Coffee

THIS SWEET COFFEE WITH A PUNCH was often served as an after-dinner drink at dinner parties at the Compound, especially in the colder months. In Ireland, instead of topping the drink with a dollop of whipped cream, they float thick cold cream on top of the hot coffee.

FOR EACH DRINK:

1 cup good strong coffee
2 teaspoons light brown sugar
1 ounce (2 tablespoons) Jameson's Irish Whiskey
Whipped cream, for garnish

POUR THE COFFEE into a heatproof stemmed glass or mug. Add the brown sugar and stir to dissolve. Pour in the Irish whiskey and top with a spoonful of whipped cream. Serve hot.

For Neil, A great chef who is equally at home cooking for the Senate and cooking for Ireland! The Taoiseach never had better fare than your Cape Cod specials.
With thanks and best wishes
Ted Kennedy April 89

Thank-you note from Senator Kennedy for all the cooking Neil did when the Irish prime minister visited the Compound in 1989.

Edward M. Kennedy

December 23, 1986

Dear Neil:

Thanks for keeping us well-fed and happy!

Warm Christmas wishes and Happy New Year.

Best,

Ted

Index

Page numbers in **bold** denote recipe on this page
Page numbers in *italics* denote photograph captions.

C

L

M

N

O

P

R

S

T

V

W

Z

Acknowledgments

I wish to thank my wonderful wife, Kathy, for her understanding all these years of the time commitments imposed upon a chef. To you I owe everything.

And Susan Wyler—a true professional with great vision.

Photo Credits

BEN FINK: Food photography, including bottom photos on front cover, photo on spine, and center photo on back cover. Also, images on contents page and on top of page 37, and full-page photographs on pages 221, 28, 39, 42, 47, 52, 55, 56, 69, 79, 80, 91, 92, 105, 108, 112, 121, 124, 129, 130, 137, 141, 147, 151, 161, 162, 166, 169, 174, 181, 184, 193, 196, 200, 208, 218, 221, 222, 235, 238, and 243.

STEVE CONNOLLY: Top photo on front cover, right photo on back cover, title page spread, all chapter opening spreads, including pages 18-19, 44-45, 72-73, 100-101, 134-135, 158-159, 182-183, and 204-205, and images on pages 8, 9, 10, 11, 16, 17, 24, 25, 36, 37 bottom, 48, 49 top and bottom, 61, 65, 84, 85, 96, 110, 111 top, 132, 172, 173, 202, 207, 212, 213top, 215, 228.

JERRY SCHMEER: Left photo on back cover and images on pages 88, 89, 122, 123, 171, 189, 198, 199 top and bottom, and 229 bottom.

SANTIAGO BAEZ: Portrait of Neil Connolly at left on page 13 and photograph of chocolate box with pulled sugar rose on page 226.

AP IMAGES: Photographs on page 7, left and right, on page 26, and on page 64.

AP IMAGES/MIKE F. KULLEN: Photograph on page 64.

PHOTODISC: Photograph on page 142.